Contents

CAREERS IN

ART AND DESIGN

The Kogan Page *Careers in...* series

Careers in Architecture (*5th edition*)

Careers in Art and Design (*8th edition*)

Careers in Computing and Information Technology (*new title*)

Careers in Fashion (*4th edition*)

Careers in Journalism (*8th edition*)

Careers in the Law (*8th edition*)

Careers in the Police Service (*5th edition*)

Careers in Retailing (*6th edition*)

Careers in Teaching (*7th edition*)

Careers in Television and Radio (*7th edition*)

Careers in the Theatre (*6th edition*)

Careers in the Travel Industry (*6th edition*)

Careers Using English (*new title*)

Careers Using Languages (*8th edition*)

Careers Working with Animals (*8th edition*)

CAREERS IN

ART AND DESIGN

Noel Chapman

eighth edition

First published in 1981
Eighth edition 1998

Kogan Page Limited
120 Pentonville Road
London N1 9JN

British Library Cataloguing in Publication Data

A CIP record for this book is available from the British Library.

ISBN 0 7494 2422 2

Typeset by Kogan Page Ltd
Printed and bound in Great Britain by Clays Ltd, St Ives plc

Introduction

Is this the Job for You?

- ❒ Am I sufficiently interested in the area and can I sustain this interest enough to beat growing competition for the rest of my working life? Simply, this question–should be phrased - am I passionate about art and design?
- ❒ Why do I want to work in art and design?
- ❒ Do I have talent or significant ability in an area related to art and design?
- ❒ What qualifications do I need, for how long and to what level do I wish to study?
- ❒ Do my qualifications match my aims?
- ❒ Am I self-motivated, resourceful and good at generating ideas?
- ❒ Am I good at working on my own and, equally, can I work successfully in a team?
- ❒ Can I stick to deadlines and meet professional standards of practice?

- ❐ Can I take constructive criticism yet remain focused on personal aims and objectives?

Art and design is a neat and compact title, though grossly inadequate, for the sprawling range of jobs and careers that it encompasses. Over recent years the world of art and design has expanded enormously, recognition has been given to the importance of not only having purely creative people, but also people with other skills and abilities – people who can lead, organize, coordinate, direct and manage others. The computer here, as in other spheres of contemporary life, has revolutionized the way we work, the scope and span of art and design and consequently the skills involved.

Whether you see yourself working alone as an artist designer or craftsperson, or forming part of a professional team with key roles in industry and commerce, you probably have much to learn before you feel equipped and confident enough to survive in this fast-moving and highly competitive world.

Through art and design we can experience the opportunity to combine personal and creative development. The role of the artist and designer is constantly changing and evolving as new applications of design are discovered and the boundaries of art are rolled further back. Despite enormous changes, mainly due to funding and economics, in the way that courses are structured and operated, art and design education in this country still offers a unique form of personal exploration, training and development, unlike any other programme of academic study. The range of subjects is already wide, and continually increasing. The applications are apparently limitless – from painting or conceptual art to product design, from stained glass or sculpture to computer animation.

Modern electronic media systems challenge the technical and creative abilities of the designer and we have in recent years seen the introduction of film, video, computer-aided design, desk top publishing and other computer applications in our courses. Art and design education responds to the needs of industry, by tradition, providing a vocational form of training to equip young designers and artists at the start of their careers.

This book will help to throw some light on the range of career opportunities that fall into the categories of art and design and to explain the routes through art and design education in colleges and universities in the United Kingdom.

The creative process by which artists and designers work and the skills and attributes they develop on their courses aim to prepare them for the demands of an ever-changing world. They must learn to develop critical awareness, to be self-motivated, independent, flexible, open to all possibilities, and their personal development is integral to the design process and the artefacts they produce. Whatever field of work they enter, whether in art, design, craft or in something totally unrelated, they are equipped to make a valuable contribution to the world in which we live and work. Even for those sure of the direction they wish their career to take, the route to achieving this is not always clear. Where to start? How long does the training last? What qualifications must I have? These are just some questions that arise, and which this book aims to answer.

2 Deciding on a career in art and design

Is training really necessary?

Studying art and design inevitably means spending between two and five years or more in further and higher education (see Chapter 3). Few people manage to succeed as practising artists or designers without having been through an art or design education, and natural talent is not the only consideration; art and design education in this country has developed over the years to provide the creative, theoretical, technical and personal elements that combine to equip its graduates with the basic skills and attitudes they need to begin their careers.

Often it is not until near completion of their courses that many people actually become aware of exactly where their true interests and abilities lie: when the full range of career opportunities opens up to them and what they require becomes apparent. The competitive world in which we work makes the possession of recognized qualifications increasingly important in all fields. When dealing in the currency of individualism and innovation, recognized qualifications provide prospective employers with a standard by which to gauge the level of your talents and abilities.

Which subject?

There were, at the last count, possibly 100 different course subject titles in art design, from wildlife illustration to weaving, and from knitwear design to fine art. Some courses are geared to the needs of specific industries, some may be very technical; others place a greater emphasis on artistic expression and creativity, and some may have a high academic content.

In order to examine each area in more detail, art and design is divided into the headings listed below.

1. Creative and performing arts – some combine courses with theatre, music, dance, the visual arts
2. Fashion and textiles – including embroidery, footwear, knitwear, woven, printed and knitted textiles
3. Fine art – painting, sculpture, printmaking, etc
4. Graphic design and illustration
5. History of art and design
6. Three-dimensional design – interior design, industrial and product design, wood, ceramics, furniture, silversmithing, jewellery, metal, plastics, glass
7. Other subjects related to art and design – education degrees (BEd); combined courses; film, photography, television, media studies.

Boundaries between areas can be vague or even overlap. For example, graphics students may work in three dimensions, three-dimensional students may do painting so don't expect to find courses are limited to a narrow field of study. In addition, there are some multi-disciplinary and combined courses where more than one subject area may be studied, eg a degree in three-dimensional design with graphics and textiles.

An increasingly wide range of options is offered within courses as influences and applications of art and design grow. For example, at most colleges graphic design now includes computer graphics as applied to design for television and film as well as typography and image manipulation. As complementary studies, many art and design students do drama, dance and movement, read psychology, economics, social studies, business studies, literature – an unlimited range of other options, depending on the course.

The study of the history of art and design, more usually called 'contextual studies', 'complementary studies' or 'design theories', forms an integral part of all art and design degree courses, foundation courses and most vocational courses. Art and design is not, therefore, purely practical, creative and technical. A great deal of importance is placed on the practice of art and design in the light of historical and critical studies from early movements and periods in art and architecture to the study of contemporary art, design and social issues.

Creative and performing arts

Creative and performing arts courses are mostly offered at degree level. In the past, study of music, drama and theatre arts, dance and the visual arts in higher education was taught as individual courses, often in specialized institutions such as colleges of dance or music, or on teacher-training courses. The boundaries between different forms of artistic expression in the performance and visual arts have become less well defined over the years; dance and drama are closely related as are music and movement, the visual arts and music, and so on. Creative and performing arts courses have emerged as an exciting way of exploring, at an academic and practical level, one or more of the disciplines and relationships between the different forms of expression. The combinations of subjects which art and design courses offer vary considerably, so it is best to consult the *UCAS Handbook* (see Further Reading) for a brief synopsis of course content, then if a course sounds interesting, contact the college concerned directly for more details and the course handbook.

The main constituent areas

- *visual arts* – not just drawing and painting, but these could also include sculpture, three-dimensional design or crafts such as wood or ceramics, printmaking, photography and film, graphics, textiles, and supporting theoretical and historical studies

- *theatre or drama* – can include not only practical work through performance and workshop sessions, but historical studies; technical back-up; stage management; lighting and effects; costume; creative writing
- *music* – most students are musically qualified in one or more orchestral or solo instruments, such as the violin, oboe or piano. Some courses offer greater flexibility and students may be using modern instruments such as electric guitars and keyboard instruments, and electronic music. Music will normally be supported by theoretical and historical studies
- *dance* – practical and technical aspects: choreography, dance composition, improvisation, movement studies, historical studies in dance; the use of music, costume, theatrical effects; exploration and study of styles from classical ballet to modern dance; uses of production workshops prevalent throughout; inter-relation with drama, music etc
- *other options* – one course offers arts administration, another offers English with creative writing. Some courses place an emphasis on community involvement and students may become involved with local community arts activities during their courses.

At the interview, students are expected to give evidence of their creative abilities and present a folio of recent work, if applying for visual arts.

Students opting for drama, music or dance will almost certainly be expected to prepare a piece for audition. The academic content of the courses is fairly high, and the intellectual development of the students is as important as it would be for any other academic degree course. Outside their course studies, students are expected regularly to attend concerts, theatrical productions, dance shows or ballets and visit art galleries, to complement their studies.

Fashion and textile design

Fashion and textile design courses exist at all levels of qualification – foundation, vocational, degree and postgraduate. There are normally chief studies in two main areas: *fashion design* – garment and accessory design; and *textile design, printed, knitted or woven* – for fashion or furnishing and decorative use. The fashion designer requires an understanding of textiles and their uses. The textile designer must be aware of the applications of fabrics in clothing and decorative areas. Some courses combine fashion and textiles design as the main area of study.

The courses involve creative, academic and technical aspects, for example, general design studies, professional design practice, techniques such as weaving, printing and dyeing, pattern design and cutting, sewing skills, machine and hand-knitted fabrics and clothing.

There are some courses in the fashion and textile areas which are devoted solely to one subject for specialized study, eg embroidery, design of carpets and related textiles, and knitwear design. Some courses are completely broad based and simply entitled 'Surface pattern' or such. Many offer business or management studies, including marketing, accounts, commerce, and economics. Fashion promotion, retailing and journalism are recent additions to the range of courses available. Some courses are four years long with industrial placements in relevant companies in the UK and abroad. These courses prepare students for many different careers in the fashion and textiles and related industries in design, production, promotion, management or publishing. Many designers work freelance or in small textile design studios and consultancies.

Fine art

What is fine art?

Various course brochures describe their courses in the following ways; 'chief studies in painting, fine printmaking, or sculpture!

Encourages the discovery of the nature of the student's talent by imaginative use of a wide variety of available facilities based on a personal work programme'. 'An open situation wherein any form of enquiry into perceptual expression is allowable and where students may evolve and design their own terms of their visual language.' 'An enquiry into relationships between elements, objects, space ...' One student's view:

> I followed a fine arts degree, and although I shall probably end up doing some totally unrelated job, I feel the luxury of being able to spend three years exploring myself and my ideas through my artwork has been an exciting and fulfilling experience and is something I shall always value.

What can you do in fine art?

Most fine art departments offer painting, sculpture – in a whole range of materials, printmaking – silk-screen, lithography – etching, film, video, photography and other media courses. Some departments expect you to choose one area to specialize in, while others will give you the opportunity to work in whichever area you choose. There will be a considerable amount of drawing and supporting studies to complement your main subject. You might want to work in ceramics, wood, cement, stone or fibreglass, but it is important to stress that you will not necessarily be receiving training as a craftsperson. Instruction in basic techniques and use of tools and equipment may be taught but creativity and freedom of expression with the materials are the chief aim. Film, video or photography facilities are available to most art and design students, and in some departments it is possible to choose one of these as the main area of creative study.

History and theory of art is an extremely important aspect of most fine art courses, which believe that it is essential for you to study the major art movements, including contemporary art, in order to gain an understanding of the development of art and how this may relate to your own creativity. All fine art courses will have a structure, but within that there may be tremendous freedom to explore things in depth and organize your own work programme; a high degree of self-motivation is required.

What of the career prospects? Most fine art students are aware that there are no recognized vocational ends and see the course as an intellectual and creative exercise in its own right, possibly in the same way as would a student of philosophy or other non-vocational academic degree subject. Many potential fine art students are discouraged by parents, friends, teachers and others who see no obvious vocation except that of a struggling, practising artist. But far from emerging from college as unemployable misfits, information collected by art colleges and other surveys has shown that fine art leavers enter a wide range of jobs and occupations both related and unrelated to art and design.

Graphic design and illustration

Graphic design is to do with visual communication. A number of different disciplines can fall under the broad heading of graphic design: design studies, film and animation work, typography and lettering, illustration, printing processes and printmaking, display and exhibition work, technical graphics for engineering, calligraphy, model-making, packaging, design for advertising, and so on.

Design itself is normally the chief area of study, where the student, through theory and practice, learns the basic principles of design and explores the elements of visual communication. On some courses it is possible to pursue a specialist subject such as illustration (even medical and scientific), photography and film, typography, packaging, illustration and exhibition design. The uses and application of modern technology including computers are increasingly a feature of courses. Film, TV and video courses are increasingly offered in graphic design courses.

Graphic design work is not necessarily always in two dimensions. Many students do three-dimensional studies, particularly where this is applied to model-making, packaging, exhibition design or display.

The study of the history of art and design and supporting or complementary studies comprise at least 15–20 per cent of degree courses and many include psychology, social and economic issues.

Students are encouraged to have a professional approach to their work, as would be expected of a qualified designer working in industry. The structure of courses at degree, vocational and foundation level will be geared to project-based work, working to a set 'brief', and meeting deadlines. For example, a theme for a design project may be a 'health education' campaign and, within that, students may be asked to produce a series of designs for posters, handbills and magazines advertising. Within the brief, there may be restrictions with regards to the budget available, printing facilities, deadlines to be met, and so on. On degree courses in particular, tutors may encourage students to design their own work programmes, set their own projects, topics and deadlines, the emphasis being on self-directed study. Professional studies will be fundamental to all courses and will cover aspects such as how to approach and deal with clients, how to respond to a brief, how to present work to clients, printing requirements and limitations, and gaining familiarity with the jargon used.

History of art and design

Your interest may lie in art appreciation, criticism and history rather than participating in creative artistic activity yourself. The history of art and design can be studied as an academic degree, and also features as an integral part of degree, foundation and many vocational courses in art and design.

Let us take, first of all, the history of art and design as an academic course in its own right. Some courses are purely the study of the history of design or history of art while others encompass both. Universities and colleges offer BA degrees in this range of subjects. Sometimes the history of art and design may be offered with other subsidiary or joint academic subjects, such as languages, history, literature, and so on.

Second, let us look at the history of art and design as part of an art and design degree, foundation and vocational courses. One of the myths attached to art and design courses is that they are practical and therefore an easier option to pursue than academic courses. Most tutors and art students will tell you that the demands, both creative and academic, are considerable, and that it is by no means a soft option! In universities and art colleges, the academic study of the history of art and complementary studies must amount to at least 15 per cent of the course content, while in university art and design degrees, it may be more. Most vocational and foundation courses in art and design include the study of the history of art and design as an important part of the course. Whether you choose fine art, graphics, ceramics, fashion, or any other art and design subjects, you will find history of art and design studies will support and complement your creative work.

Three-dimensional design

Courses in three-dimensional design are offered at all levels, from foundation to postgraduate, at a wide range of colleges and institutions all over the country. Overall, this area of art and design is concerned with the creation of designs in three dimensions. These can be functional objects, such as furniture, product designs and jewellery, and also sculptural and non-functional forms in wood, ceramics, glass, etc

The disciplines include: chief studies in furniture design, wood, glass, metal, ceramics, plastics, jewellery, silversmithing, industrial designs and product design. Interior design and theatre design are also offered and are discussed separately below.

The approaches to working in three dimensions vary: one course may offer chief studies in industrial design, which is closely allied to engineering, and includes technological studies. Another course may offer studies in ceramics where students concentrate on free artistic expression, and experiment through working with their materials, producing functional or decorative forms. Some courses are specifically geared towards design for commercial production; others may attract students who wish to work as individual artists or craftspeople, designing and making objects in their own studios.

Interior design

Interior design is concerned with the design of living, working and leisure space inside buildings. This can include space planning, colour schemes, the selection of materials for walls, floors, ceilings, the selection of furniture and fabrics and the design of fixtures and fittings themselves.

Interior design courses sometimes have components in common with architecture courses, while others could be linked to retail display and exhibition display. Courses will include creative, technical, and professional design elements. One student says, 'Our course is geared to professional practice, and includes the study of architectural principles too. We also study psychology and the history of art and design. We work to briefs as would any designer in professional practice.'

Theatre design

This is offered at a limited number of institutions as a main subject at degree and vocational level. This is one student's experience:

> We do projects, ie reading a play and designing a set with drawings and 3D models. Fine art studies, drawing and painting are done as supporting studies. The first year includes a lot of groundwork: blocks of time spent on costume-making, set and properties construction, woodwork, scene painting, and lighting. The rest of the course is spent doing design projects with some fieldwork with outside theatres. We study history of art and history of theatre and costume, and of course playwrights. We finish with one major design for a public performance.

Costume for stage, screen, film and television

Courses are designed specifically for students willing to pursue careers as costume designers, interpreters and supervisors of costume within the film, theatre and television industries. Many costume designers and wardrobe designers now working in those industries came from fashion backgrounds, particularly those specialising in contemporary ie non-period, work. You may find it helpful to consult Noel Chapman, *Careers in Fashion* (see Further reading).

Media, film, photography and television

These subjects may feature on many art and design courses as supporting studies, and at some colleges can also be chosen as a main option in, for example, a graphic design degree course. Media studies, film, photography, television, video and TV graphics also exist as degree and vocational courses in their own right.

A number of courses exist for those interested in the broader aspects of television, video and theatre design, where management and production are also studied. Some courses mix film history and cultural studies, under such fashionable titles as media studies, lens-based media, or suchlike. Carefully study the *UCAS Handbook* (see Further reading) to find a course that offers the areas of study closest to your particular interest.

Foundation courses will usually include short courses in the use of camera and photographic techniques and may offer film, TV and photography as study areas. These areas are beyond the scope of this book and further details are given in *Careers in Television and Radio*, published by Kogan Page (see Further reading). Lists of courses at all levels are produced by the British Institute of Professional Photography and the British Film Institute. See also *Education and Training for Film and Television*, published by the British Kinematograph, Sound and Television Society.

Other subjects related to art and design

Training for teaching after completion of an art and design degree is discussed in chapter 5. However, there are other routes to becoming qualified as a teacher. One way is to follow a BEd (Bachelor of Education) degree course which is a three-or four-year training in education theory and practice for entry into the teaching profession. Art and design is offered as a main or subsidiary subject in many colleges running such courses. However, a BA in art and design concentrates more time on the pursuit of art and design for its own sake. Then, should you decide to enter teaching, the BA may be followed by a one-year postgraduate course which qualifies you to teach in schools and further education institutions. The BEd route may be shorter if you intend to teach, although you are likely to achieve more intensive art training taking a BA in art and design, followed by the one-year postgraduate teacher training courses ATC or postgraduate certificate of education (PGCE).

Those completing a course of teacher training are expected to have GCSE level passes at grade C or above in English language and maths.

3 Studying art and design

Qualifications available

Many of the qualifications listed below require full-time study. yet BTEC National Certificates and Higher National Certificates offer the opportunity to study on a part-time basis usually while in a relevant occupation. A few universities and art institutions are now offering degree level courses in art and design on a part-time basis. The qualifications available in art and design are:

- foundation courses
- BTEC Ordinary Diplomas and Certificates, Higher National Diplomas and Certificates
- professional qualifications
- diploma in Higher Education
- degrees, postgraduate degrees and advanced study.

General National Vocational Qualifications (GNVQs) are new alternatives to GCE A-level study or more GCSEs. Advanced GNVQs – the new 'vocational A-Levels' – are equivalent to two GCE A-Levels, and normally take two years' full-time study. Intermediate GNVQs are equivalent to four or five GCSEs at grades A–C, and normally take one year full-time study. Foundation GNVQs are equivalent to four GCSEs at grades D–G, and normally take one year full-time study. You can take a full GNVQ along with other qualifications – such as a GCE A-Level, AS courses, a couple of GCSEs or additional GNVQ units.

Foundation courses

Most degree and some vocational courses require students to have completed a foundation course, though those with at least two A-Levels or GNVQ equivalents (and an impressive portfolio) may be exempted by the college (except in Scotland, where foundation studies are included in full-time vocational and degree courses).

Foundation courses give a broad education in the basic elements as preparation for entry to further training on degree and vocational courses. They also enable students to test out their commitment to the subject before embarking on a full-time course for a further three or four years.

Entry requirements

For the 2-year course, the minimum age is 16. A general education is required. For the foundation course, some colleges specify GCSE grade 3 passes or equivalent. For the 1-year course, the minimum age is 17. A general education is required. For the foundation course, five GCSE grade 3 passes or equivalent; some colleges also prefer at least one A-level subject; or GNVQ equivalent.

Each applicant will normally be called for interview, with their portfolio which gives evidence of artistic or design ability.

As an alternative to foundation studies at 16+, applicants without the minimum entry requirements may apply for BTEC National Diplomas.

Vocational courses

Vocational courses in art and design provide chiefly professional and practical training in art and design subjects, as opposed to the more academic approach of degrees in art and design. Most vocational students attend courses in their own locality, since few local authorities will make awards for such courses outside their area, whereas degree students are eligible for a mandatory grant wherever they choose to study.

Entry requirements

16+ years BTEC First Diploma/Certificate – no formal entry requirements.
16+ years BTEC Ordinary National Diploma/ Certificate – 4 GCSE grade C or above passes or equivalent.
18+ years BTEC Higher National Diploma/Certificates an appropriate BTEC National Award or Foundation course and/or 4/5 GCSE grade C or above passes plus 1 A-level pass or GNVQ.

Length of courses: certificates, two years part-time; diplomas, two years full-time, three years part-time or sandwich study.

BTEC and SCOTVEC National Diplomas and Certificates

There are over 400 art and design courses at 135 colleges all over the UK, offering nationally recognized qualifications called BTEC National Diplomas and Certificates approved by the Design Board for the Business and Technology Education Council. The aim of BTEC is to offer employment-related courses in art and design studies to complement the existing provision of degree courses. The standards are high and because employers have been involved in designing the contents of the courses, there are often more practical projects. Subjects include:

- Art and Design
- Visual Communication (including graphic design, illustration, technical illustration, typography, photography, audio-visual studies, advertising design, information design)
- Fashion Textiles and Surface Patterns
- Millinery
- Footwear.

Diplomas are more advanced than Certificates which offer part-time study for those already working in design posts. It is possible to progress from a Diploma to a Higher Diploma which offers an advanced, specialist training for a further two years.

Length of courses. Two years, part-time; Diplomas: two years, full-time, three years, part-time or sandwich study. In Scotland, the Scottish Vocational Education Council (SCOTVEC) offers two-year National and Higher National Diploma courses with equivalent entry requirements to BTEC courses.

BTEC Higher National Diploma in Design

Most BTEC awards of specialism, eg Design (Fashion) courses are listed below under their area of specialism. The list shows a selection of the courses available. A full list of approved design courses can be obtained from: BTEC Information Services, Central House, Upper Woburn Place, London WC1H OHH; tel: 0171 413 8400.

Entry requirements: BTEC NC *or* ND in a related subject area, or its identifiable equivalent, *or a* BTEC ND *or* NC in General Art and Design *or* completion of a Foundation course in Art and Design *or* an A-Level pass with appropriate GCSEs.

SCOTVEC HNC

Courses available are: Arts Administration; Arts Management; Art and Design; Fine Art; Graphic Design; Graphic Reproduction; Graphics and Illustration; Interior Design; Scientific and Technical Graphics; Public Art; Spatial Design; Spatial Design(Interior Design); Spatial Design (Retail Design); Technical Graphics.

SCOTVEC HND

Arts Administration; Arts Management; Graphic Design; Graphics and Illustration; Interior Design; Spatial Design; Spatial Design (Interior Design); Spatial Design (Retail Design); Technical Graphics.

A range of National Certificate Modules is available within this sector. Certificate Modules are offered at a variety of centres.

National Council for Vocational Qualifications

NVQs are offered in:

- Level 2: Exhibition Design; Fashion Design; Furniture Design; Graphic Design; Interior Design.
- Level 3: Design.
- Level 4: Design.

City and Guilds

Courses available are: Creative Studies: Preparing Working Designs, plus one of the following craft options: Soft Furnishing; Upholstery; Fashion; Embroidery; Sugarcraft; Flower Arranging; Machine Knitting; Hand Knitting; Interior Decorative Techniques; Ceramics; Patchwork and Quilting; Lacemaking; Crochet; GNVQ in Art and Design.

RSA Examinations Board

Art and design GNVQ (available at foundation, intermediate and advanced levels).

The Royal Academy Schools

For details, contact the Royal Academy of Arts, Burlington House, Piccadilly, London WIV ODS, tel: 0171 439 7438. The RA Schools award the Royal Academy Schools Postgraduate Diploma. The course lasts for three years full-time in Fine Art, Painting and Sculpture. Candidates for the postgraduate course must have a BA Hons degree or a university degree in Fine Arts.

Professional qualifications

Some professional qualifications may be awarded after a special exam, others by completing a college course satisfactorily. Some of the professional qualifications associated with art and design are:

- CSD – Chartered Society of Designers
- LSDC – Licentiate of the Society of Designer Craftsmen

- ABID – Associateship of the British Institute of Interior Design
- BDS – British Display Society
- ATI – Associateship of the Textile Institute.

Degree courses

Degrees are offered by individual universities, art colleges, colleges of higher education and certain other institutions. These are normally three-year full-time courses leading to BA, a BA (Hons), and in one case a Bachelor of Fine Art (BFA), in art and design subjects. Some four-year MA and BA sandwich courses also exist.

Minimum academic qualifications are five GCSE grade 3 passes; or three GCSE grade 3 passes plus one A-Level pass or equivalents; or two GCSE grade 3 and two A-Level passes (or Scottish equivalents). For those who have not completed a foundation courses, minimum academic requirements may be at least two A-Level passes, GNVQ equivalents, plus O-Levels. Completion of other qualifications such as BTEC Diplomas and Certificates is acceptable, but it is wise to check with individual institutions.

The academic requirements listed here are the minimum, and many applicants to degree courses now have to achieve two A-Levels, but unqualified mature applicants, may be accepted for degree courses.

Postgraduate and advanced study

Postgraduate and advanced courses are offered in a wide range of subjects. The entry requirements are normally completion of a first degree, though some courses will accept vocational and professional qualifications. Courses lead to certificates and diplomas, or to higher degrees such as MA, MPhil, or PhD. Postgraduate study falls into two distinct areas, the first extends your art education, perhaps specializing in one particular field, eg illustration, sculpture, furniture; the second comprises courses which equip you for entry to special occupations, such as art teaching, art therapy, arts administration, normally adding a professional year to your first degree qualification.

Mature students

It is not always necessary for mature entrants to have the minimum academic requirements for entry to courses, provided they can show they have the ability and creative potential to do the course. Some mature applicants may be required to do a test, or write an essay, in addition to attending an interview.

Some colleges may encourage mature applicants to acquire one or two GCSE or A-Levels or GVNQ equivalent in art and design or in other subjects before applying, particularly if they are in doubt about the applicants' motivation and ability to cope with the demands of the course if they have been outside full-time education for some time.

How and when to apply for courses

The Universities and Colleges Admissions Service (UCAS) (see Useful addresses) is the central agency that acts on behalf of the UK universities and colleges of higher education to process applications for entry to their first degree, Diploma of Higher Education, HND and some university diploma courses.

You may have to apply almost a whole academic year in advance for courses in art and design. Most courses begin in Autumn. Dates and times given below refer to the academic year preceding the year of entry to courses.

The *UCAS Handbook,* available free from UCAS, outlines in full the application procedure and has comprehensive lists of colleges and universities and the courses they offer. Full information about courses should be obtained from prospectuses obtainable from colleges directly or contact them on the Internet. Your present school or college should also be able to advise on procedures and many hold information and prospectuses.

Foundation and vocational courses in art and design: 1 year and 2 year courses

Write to your local education authority at the Education Office, asking for details of their courses, and then apply to the colleges in which you are interested. You will probably be called for an interview and asked to bring a portfolio of your work.

When to apply: (normally to your local art college) autumn to spring. Some popular courses are full by January, so be sure to apply in good time. No final closing date.

Method of application: application forms from the college(s) to which forms are returned direct.

Degree courses and BTEC higher diplomas in art and design

The closing date for applications through UCAS is 15 December, but there are a couple of exceptions; Oxford – 15 October and college entrance form by 30 September, (Ruskin School) Oxbridge 15 October.

Postgraduate study: higher degrees and diplomas in art and design

When to apply: forms available beginning of January. To be returned not later than end of January.

Method of application: application forms from your own college, or if you have already left, obtain direct from UCAS.

Postgraduate Art Teachers' Certificate/Diploma 1 year

When to apply: mid-October.

Postgraduate Certificate in Education (PGCE)

When to apply: October onwards of year prior to entry.

Interviews

Your motivation, your interest in the subject and the college or university, your suitability for the course, your abilities and your portfolio are all taken into account. It is important to prepare for the interview by finding out as much as you can about the college, the course content, methods of tuition and assessment, facilities, options and subject choices. Open Days will give you the opportunity to talk to students and staff and look around. At some colleges, particularly at postgraduate level, you may be required to do an entrance test or exam.

The style of the interview will vary from college to college. At one you may be interviewed in a group along with other applicants, while at another you may talk individually with tutors. Whatever the policy, you will be asked to talk about your work and to show that you are fairly sure in your own mind about doing that particular course. Beforehand, you should find someone who can help you prepare for the interview, by selecting work, and discussing the questions you should ask.

Grants

The grants position for many students is at present uncertain, owing to cuts in local authority budgets. Some LEAs are restricting the number and type of awards given to students. It is essential that you find out early on about your eligibility for an award and the kind of grant you may receive. You should make a grant application to your LEA in the spring *even* if you have not yet been accepted onto a course. Many LEAs like to receive grant applications by the *end of March* for entry to courses the following year.

Here is a rough guide to the current grant position for most of the art and design courses.

- *Discretionary award.* This means that the LEA is not obliged to give you an award and if they do, the amount may vary according to how the LEA views the course. Travel awards are also discretionary.

- *Mandatory awards.* This means that the LEA is obliged to give you a major award for post A-Level, ie further education courses, provided that you are eligible in all other respects.
- *Foundation courses.* Discretionary. Many LEAs will not consider financing you outside their area.
- *Vocational courses.* Discretionary. Many LEAs will not consider financing you outside their area unless the course you wish to do is *not* offered by their own colleges. The type of grant you are awarded may vary. Your LEA should be able to tell you the designation of your course and the type of award you might be eligible for.
- *Degree, DipHE and BTEC Higher Diplomas.* Mandatory. Students are normally eligible for a major award.
- *Postgraduate Teacher Training Courses (ATC) (PGCE).* Students are normally eligible for an award from their LEA.
- *Postgraduate Courses – Higher Degrees, Diplomas, Certificates.* For some courses of study you may qualify for a postgraduate bursary or studentship from the Department for Education and Employment. You should apply for nomination through your postgraduate college at the time you apply for the course. Otherwise, grants are awarded at the discretion of your LEA, or there may be scholarships awarded by the colleges to which you are applying. Some postgraduate courses will allow you to register as a part-time student, over a long period, and you will be able to support yourself with a part-time job. The course to which you are applying will tell where you should seek finance.

Loans

Many would-be students for whom grants are not available are turning to other students, for a loan. Terms vary slightly but the deal is usually that you begin repayments to the Student Loans Company (see Useful addresses), normally by direct debit, in 60 instalments over five years, starting the April after you finish the course. Payments can be deferred if you earn less than 85 per cent of the national average wage.

Repayment of government education grants usually begins three years after finishing further education; the repayment arrangements depend upon your earnings, and can be deferred if circumstances warrant.

Where to study

The list of colleges and universities and the courses offered is now so great it cannot be included within the scope of this book. A list of directories and reference books is given in Further Reading where you will find in particular the *UCAS Handbook* very useful and comprehensive. Most public libraries and schools, colleges or careers libraries hold up-to-date information. Many colleges publish their prospectuses on the Internet.

You also consult the *Directory of Further Education Courses* (published by CRAC), the *Postgraduate Directory of Graduate Studies* (CRAC) and *British Qualifications* published by Kogan Page. The addresses and phone numbers of these organizations can be found under Useful addresses.

Regional Advisory Councils for Further Education produce regional guides to courses in art and design. If you are making initial enquiries about first diplomas or foundation courses, ask at your school or local careers office. Professional organizations supply lists of recommended courses, for example, the Textiles Institute publishes a list of textile courses.

Information provided was correct at the time of writing, but do allow for changes, and check that there have not been any changes before taking action. Entry qualifications, particularly for vocational courses, vary from college to college. These may be checked by obtaining individual prospectuses.

4 Occupations and jobs available

Artists and designers go on to enter a wide variety of occupations after leaving college. Some art and design centres keep detailed information about the occupations entered by their students after college, and if you wish to find out more, you could contact individual departments or college career advisers.

General career prospects

So what do art school-leavers do?

- They go on to *further study* in art and design, or further professional training, such as arts administration and art therapy (see Chapter 5) or apply to the various government enterprise programmes and allowance schemes to start up as a potential small business.
- They enter one-year courses of *teacher training* as specialist art teachers in secondary schools or as primary school teachers.
- They find temporary work, often unrelated to art, while trying to establish themselves in *self-employment*, including freelancing, setting up a craft workshop, and consultancy.
- They enter *art and design-related jobs*, for example, an assistant art editor on a magazine, a ceramic designer in industry, a graphic designer in a design consultancy, a mural artist on an arts project.

- They go into jobs where their *art and design background* is useful – such as in *exhibition* and *museum work*, as *advertising account executive*, *retail buying*, or *arts administration*.
- They enter *occupations open to all graduates*, regardless of subject – in retail management, administration, tourism, and leisure or even accountancy and computing.
- They *travel abroad* to broaden their experience.

In general, the more highly qualified you are, the more likely you are to find a job. The achievement of a degree or diploma in itself, together with other personal skills and interests, may combine to equip artists and designers for careers in many fields, both related and unrelated to their course of study. For many art students, the opportunity to spend three or four years at college may have been an end in itself, an important stage in their personal development.

What are the prospects?

The economic successes of the early 1980s changed for ever the way design and designers were perceived. Companies realized that good design sells, the term 'designer' in relation to a product was coined, as in designer clothes, designer perfume, etc. Customers became design aware and more willing to pay for what they believed to be a better quality product. Manufacturers have also learnt the importance of design, that design sells, and when you think of their sponsorship of the arts it is obvious that industry saw that art also had cachet.

The effect of this awareness spread into other areas of industry and now many forward-thinking companies realize the benefits of having designer or managers of sales and production people with design backgrounds. While it would be misleading to simply say that employment prospects have improved for art and design graduates, the broadening of the range of jobs now available does present a more positive situation. However, jobs are no less competitive in a world where people are becoming better qualified.

Postgraduate study

For some advanced courses it is often desirable for applicants to have developed their work independently for at least one year after leaving art school. Funding for postgraduate study has diminished over the years, though many students find they can get industrial sponsorship in return for freelance work. Increasingly, in response to the shortage of finance, many postgraduate centres now accept applicants on a part-time basis for higher degrees and advanced diploma courses.

What skills do artists and designers need to survive after college?

First of all they should look at their own personal needs. Then at their skills and interests. What kind of lifestyle do they want – in the short term and the long term? In addition, they need to be:

- well informed
- realistic
- self-motivated
- adaptable to change
- flexible
- persistent
- creative beyond their degree
- professional and able to see art in a wider context.

Recreating a college environment, by establishing a network of friends and contacts, grouping together with others, sharing skills and experiences, and joining artists' and designers' organizations, can help to counter feelings of isolation after college. Most importantly, artists need to assess their skills and find ways of using these other settings after college. See Chapter 6 for 'Top tips for getting into the industry'.

Creative and performing arts jobs

Depending on their interests, graduates from these courses may be well equipped to enter postgraduate study in a specialized field, such as theatre management, arts administration, the visual arts, art history, or may go on to further professional training in dance, drama, or music. Relevant occupations may include: teaching after a one-year postgraduate course; arts administration, in galleries, theatre, music, regional arts associations; in television, radio, and film as researchers, performers, designers, production assistants; in community arts, particularly where the course has a strong community element; youth and community work; work in magazine and book publishing; journalism; in visual art and design; or work as performers in dance, drama or music.

Fashion and textile designers

Most fashion and textile design students hope to seek an occupation related to their training. They may have studied from a range of options: fashion design, footwear design, carpet design, furnishing textiles, fashion textiles, embroidery, knitted and printed textiles, weaving, and so on. Some courses also include business administration elements which may lead to careers in management in the fashion and textiles industries.

Many students specializing in fashion design or in textiles for fashion hope to find work as design assistants in the studios and workrooms of fashion companies, from well-known 'designer names' (where few posts exist), right down to the popular end of the market with the mass-produced interpretations of current trends.

A designer needs to be well informed, and many spend a considerable amount of time researching, visiting shows of fashion collections and trade fairs, talking to buyers and marketing staff. Designs are not the products of pure inspiration. A combination of creative talent and an understanding and awareness of the market of production and business problems is essential. Many graduates go into retail as sales assistants where they then progress to buying, marketing and merchandising jobs.

Case Study

***Andrew** left the Royal College of Art eight years ago.*

'I was always interested in fashion and left school at 16 to take a GAD National Diploma course with a fashion specialization. At 18 I was accepted on to the BA (Hons) degree course at Nottingham Trent Polytechnic. I felt I needed more time to develop my work and made a successful application to the RCA.'

Andrew won a number of national and international awards and competitions while a student, and also worked both freelance and on placement during vacations as a designer and pattern cutter, the work varying between suppliers of mass market or high street stores in Britain and a high fashion designer label in Italy.

'On leaving the RCA at the age of 23, I was immediately offered a job in Germany working for an international fashion company. I turned this job down in favour of a job in England which offered broader experience working for a manufacturer supplying mass market multiples. The job involved fabric selection, liaising with buyers, creating and presenting theme boards, designing and personally cutting the selected designs, as well as overseeing the sample room production. From here I moved on to a designer at Alexon International where my work was varied and challenging. I worked within a large team, and became responsible for designing day and evening dresses and soft suitings. The work involved compiling theme and mood boards for each season, selecting a colour palette, researching and liaising with both UK and international fabric agents as well as designing.

'After doing specific drawings for the sample room, I would then oversee the garments at toile stage, taking responsibility for the correct pads, buttons, trims and so on. Finished garments were delivered to me before I presented them to my design executive.

'I was heavily involved in pricing meetings, fittings and organizing the finished range for the press shows and photographic shoots.'

A few years later, after moving on to other similar jobs and having completed several prestigious freelance commissions, Andrew decided the time was right to embark on a long-term dream to team up with an ex-colleague from his days at Nottingham, Reynold Pierce.

Reynold's career had followed similar lines: an MA at Central St Martin's led to a design job with John Galliano, other industrial experience and, again, exciting freelance commissions. With an enormous amount of experience under their belts Andrew and Reynold thought they would complement each other perfectly and formed the label *Pierce Fionda*. They used all their joint resources and charm to raise finance and negotiate good deals for showing and selling their collections with the right people, contacts made while in employment. They were an instant success – so much so that they had to close their order books. This was only part of it. Then they had to get the clothes made to standard and delivered on time, and this is where their backgrounds really paid off.

They see their periods in employment as a kind of apprenticeship. This knowledge and their experience are helping to underpin their future which, judging from their success of their follow-up collections, is looking very rosy. In autumn 1995 they were chosen as 'New Generation Designers of the Year' by the British Fashion Council. They have won subsequent awards each year since.

Fashion illustrators

This is an area where, traditionally, specific training has not existed. Most successful illustrators trained as fashion designers by way of degree courses. Most people will confirm that, having gone through the rigours of conventional, design-based degree courses, the would-be illustrator not only has a rounded view of the whole industry and the illustrator's role within it, but also a sound understanding of garment construction, fabrics and the body. However, in response to the growing interest in this area, a number of colleges are now offering fashion illustration options. For more information, see Noel Chapman, Careers in Fashion (see Further Reading).

Case Study

***Hilary** is a freelance illustrator.*

Hilary took a two-year Fine Arts course at Ahmadu Bello University in Nigeria where her parents were then working. This was recognized as a foundation course and back in England she was able to enter the second year at Bradford College of Art, starting in textiles but changing mid-course to fashion, concentrating on drawing. She realized that she wanted to specialize in fashion illustration so, after qualifying, she took a one-year advanced course at Central St Martin's.

Her first job was with Nigel French (Forecast/Design Consultancy) where she stayed for ten years illustrating monthly retail reports, design forecasts, knitwear reports and special design projects for manufacturers in Australia, the USA, Canada, Japan and South Africa. The work involved regular visits to Paris, Milan, Florence and Rome to cover press shows, trade fairs and shops, gathering information, then illustrating after returning to London. Having made quite a few contacts through small illustration jobs, Hilary eventually decided to become freelance and now operates from her home studio, working mainly for design consultancies and companies such as Marks and Spencer, Courtaulds, Burton Groups and IWS, plus a small amount of magazine work. She continues to travel to European fashion centres and to New York fairly frequently for one or two of the smaller consultancies.

She enjoys the freedom of choosing her own hours of work but the tight deadlines and the chasing of clients for overdue payments can sometimes be very frustrating.

Hilary enjoys being freelance and working at home and doesn't miss the tedium of daily commuting.

Textile designers

As there are few full-time jobs in the UK for textile designers – most of the big textile companies being based abroad – most textile designers in Britain either work for small design studios who sell work on to clients or they work freelance and sell their work through studios and agents. Some textiles designers work as designers or craftspeople, designing and producing their own work for exhibition, direct sale, or through limited retail craft outlets.

Textile design includes printed, knitted and woven textiles for garments, for household use, for furnishings or sometimes for decoration, as wall hangings, for example. There are ancillary areas, such as embroidery, lace and trimmings.

Case Study

***Sue** is a freelance textile designer and agent.*

Sue completed a foundation course near her home in the North West following this up with a three-year degree at Nottingham Trent University where she specialized in printed textiles. She then went on to complete a further one and a half-year MA course at Birmingham (now the University of Central England). 'This enabled me to experiment further with printing techniques and design concepts suitable for both the fashion and furnishing industries.'

This in itself was unusual as textile designers usually specialize in one area or the other. Sue then moved to London where she worked for three different design studios, learning how to adapt her ideas for the commercial market, and about the different requirements of the printed textile industry around the world.

After four years' training in the industry (this is how she saw her employment), she felt she had enough experience to produce design collections independently and teamed up with a partner from a fashion background. They designed, manufactured and marketed their own collection for a couple of years before deciding to concentrate on 'the designs themselves' and allow larger manufacturers to concentrate on the production.

The print design studio is run from Sue's home in London. She herself designs and acts as an agent for 12 freelance designers in Australia, Europe, Scandinavia, and uses an additional agent to represent her studio in the USA and Japan.

The collection consists of one-off fashion prints suitable for all areas of the industry, eg menswear, dress, swimwear, sportswear, and children's wear. The turn-over of ideas is tremendous as each designer is constantly working on new techniques, print processes, colour combinations and imagery to make the collection innovative yet commercial.

'We work one and a half years ahead of what is seen in the shops. This allows the converters to purchase prints, have the base cloths dyed and printed and available for the fashion designer to use for their collections.'

The team has been carefully selected from the graduation shows over a five-year period to vary and enrich the collection.

'As we cater for such a diverse market, we have to incorporate a real variety within the collection. I now feel the balance is just right between the creativity of designing and the excitement of selling these concepts all over the world.'

Case Study

Sally and Kim *sold their fashion designs direct to the public on a stall at Covent Garden and now run a furnishing fabric company.*

Sally and Kim trained as textile artists and started applying this to clothes. They designed a range of hand-painted shirts and dresses. They started off getting orders by making appointments with fashionable shops, which led them to a concession in a smart shop with branches in Bond Street and Hampstead. This worked well initially, but the shops went into liquidation and they were left with debts.

This setback prompted them to look into the possibility of selling their work directly to the public through a market stall at Covent Garden. They would recommend this method as an excellent way to start a business for the following reasons:

- You get immediate feedback on your work and can increase production on popular lines, while still being able to experiment with new designs or follow trends.
- Cash flow: outgoings are kept low, and customers pay when items are sold rather than the credit that shops ask for.
- Prices are better. Shops mark up at least 117.5 per cent and often up to 100 per cent.

The business outgrew the stall and they sold to major retailers such as Paul Smith, Jones, Harvey Nichols and major stores in the USA.

Sally and Kim would urge caution as far as expenditure on trade shows are concerned; this expense, combined with bulk production costs, and the possible delays in payments from shops, affects cash flow and reduces profits.

They stopped working in the fashion business in 1988 after realizing that, for them, their homeware products were more rewarding and satisfying. They now run a successful furnishing fabric company.

Freelance designers

On leaving college, some graduates successfully support themselves on a freelance basis working from home or in their own studios – possibly producing designs commissioned or bought by agents, clothing manufacturers, or furnishing or fashion textiles manufacturers directly. Some manage to set up their own small businesses where they design and produce garments on a small scale through their own shops, by mail order, or through a limited number of retail outlets.

Fine artists

Fine art graduates do not necessarily expect to incorporate their fine art into future employment. 'I have no wish to include my art – except my artistic sense – in my work, and although it remains a very important part of my life, and I still practise, it remains a private thing,' says one ex-student. For many, the course may have been an end in itself.

But it is clear that some have set out from college with the aim of developing their work, possibly seeking commissions, selling work to galleries, and arranging individual and group shows of their work. After leaving college it may take, at the earliest, six months to complete sufficient work in order to exhibit and to be successful in applying for grants and bursaries. There may be periods of unemployment or part-time and temporary work to achieve this end. The lack of studio space, college facilities and money with which to live and buy materials are often obstacles to be overcome, but a few who are determined do survive.

After college, fine artists enter a wide variety of occupations, often following a different job and pursuing their art at home. Art teaching seems an obvious occupation, as a way of maintaining an involvement with work while earning a living, but in recent years job opportunities have declined and salaries have dropped.

A few enter 'graduate' occupations in management roles – in occupations which are regularly entered by graduates from other arts disciplines such as history, philosophy, and languages. Others are known to obtain posts or seek further training in arts administration, museums and art galleries, community arts, art therapy, and in design areas – advertising, graphics and illustration, carpet and textile design, scenic design in television, art restoration and conservation.

Graphic designers

After leaving college, graphic designers find work in design consultancies; in advertising agencies; in magazine and book publishing; in television and film companies; with printers; with in-house design groups in industrial and commercial companies; in education; in museums art galleries and art organizations; in local authorities and government departments. With the skills they have acquired at college, designers may specialize in graphic design, magazine design, packaging, photography, illustration, audio-visual materials, technical graphics, display and exhibition design, or typography. (A typographer is concerned with choosing the right typeface or lettering for a piece of art work.) Of course, many designers will need skills in some or all of these areas in any one job.

Advertising agencies are major employers of graphic designers. Their work may involve visualizing ideas for packaging, television advertising, point-of-sale display, and so on, and the designer will need to be competent in all graphic design skills, though in the larger advertising agencies specialists such as typographers and photographers may be employed. The designer must be able to work as a member of a team, often under pressure to meet deadlines.

Case Study

***Stephen** is an art director with an advertising agency.*

Stephen, a graphic student, entered as a trainee art director with a large advertising agency where he learnt the basic art direction skills, technical skills, how advertising works, and also travelled abroad to visit other agencies. After a year he was offered a post of art director with another agency, and after a further six months moved to a larger agency. He felt that these frequent moves early in his career were natural for him, but others may stay longer in their first job.

'My job is art director. The job entails devising advertisements for press or television, and seeing them through to their printed or televised stage. After the idea is approved, a photographer or illustrator is hired (or a director for a commercial) by the art director to complete the art work. Copy is set as briefed, and mechanicals (the finished art work ready for reproduction) for print production made up. The art director oversees all these processes and is responsible for the finished look of the ad. This is a creatively satisfying job, and unlike some areas of the art world, money is not a problem when producing work. The job is also financially very rewarding. I intend to continue to gain experience as an art director and hope to do more television work in the future.'

Design consultancies

Design consultancies are independent firms of designers employing several different kinds of designer: graphic, package, product, display, exhibition, textile, furniture, interior designers, and many others who undertake major and minor design jobs for industrial and commercial companies. For example, a new prestige book shop is opening shortly. The owner brings in the design consultancy to design the shop interior, all point-of-sale display fittings and all business stationery to be used – from sale wrapping paper to company invoices and sales slips. When the shop is due to open, the design team work on the promotion and publicity material and press advertisements. Some design studios and consultancies, however, may be more specialized in their approach, offering, for example, purely graphic design and publicity services. Colin, a graphic designer, said,

> I find working in a design consultancy extremely stimulating. There is such a cross-fertilisation of ideas, with so many different designers working together and the scope of work can be so varied. One day I might be designing simple letterheads. Another, I might be the member of a design team looking at the problems associated with an international company wishing to update its image – its advertising materials, its stationery, the layout and interior of its premises and so on.

Addresses of design consultancies and of professional designers are maintained by the Chartered Society of Designers (see Useful Addresses). A register of designers' services appears every month in *Design* magazine.

Designers in publishing

Book publishers and magazine publishing houses employ graphic designers as art assistants and art directors. The art director or designer is responsible for the overall visual appearance of the book or magazine which they carry out in consultation with the editorial staff. This may involve choosing appropriate typefaces, deciding on the layout of page or book covers, and the overall design, often employing the services of freelance illustrators and photographers for the necessary visual extras.

Case Study

***Nicky** worked as a graphic designer for a publisher.*

At 18 Nicky completed a BTEC National Diploma in general art and design, with a strong portfolio in drawing and, having gained an introduction to a range of art and design disciplines, she chose to pursue a degree course in Visual Communications at Bath (now Graphic Design BA Hons). She was sure at once that this suited her.

'The course had a varied and exciting first year with drawing, graphic design, animation, time-based media, photography and illustration. I was encouraged to explore my potential in all these areas and could choose either a multi-option final year or a more specific route.

'My continuing fascination with drawing led me towards illustration and on completion of my degree I was accepted on a year's honorary postgraduate fellowship in Printmaking and Papermaking. This was structured by myself with the use of workshops and a free studio. The following summer I taught Papermaking at a summer school in France.

'After four years studying in Bath I moved to London to start a part-time postgraduate course in illustration at Central St Martin's. This offered advice from working illustrators, "live projects" and a place to discuss ideas and learn more about the business of illustration. I started working freelance. After a couple of years, I realized the isolated lifestyle of an illustrator did not suit me, coupled with a hard financial struggle within a depressed economic climate.

'With a lifelong interest in books I started working part-time as a traditional paste-up artist for a small press – Redstone Press – producing art books and a diary each year. After this apprenticeship I wanted to become more involved in the design process and applied to work at Dorling Kindersley – a large, international publishers renowned for its Eye Witness children's series of books and its innovative use of photography and illustration. I learnt a lot during this period, working closely with the author as part of a team of designers and editors, working to a budget and schedule, researching and collating information from outside organizations for image reference, liaising with picture researchers, ordering and selecting transparencies. I designed spreads from initial ideas to final layouts and ready to print, visualizing art works, models and photography. The book could also involve art directing shoots and buying props. Designers have to keep to production deadlines, liaising with the production department and colour correcting proofs. I learnt to use QuarkXPress and other Mac programs, a skill that had eluded me until this point!

'After completing a number of books I saw a job teaching graphic design part-time on a foundation course. I was looking for a new challenge and change of direction. It was an opportunity to return some of my knowledge to education and I enjoy the intellectual stimulation and the diversity of my job.

'Interesting work and having a satisfying and creative life are my motivating factors, huge financial rewards have never been a goal. Working freelance enables me to change my work direction or combine a variety of jobs in the art and design field.'

Freelance graphic designers

Few graphic designers attempt full-time freelance work or set up their own design studios immediately on leaving college, though after only one or two years in employment they may do so, when they have sufficient commercial experience to be able to understand and interpret the needs of the clients, to organize and run their own business and to set up their own studio. The section on freelance illustration has many points in common with the work of the designer.

Graphic designers in television

The work of the graphics department in a television company is extremely wide-ranging. It includes typography, lettering, doing simple credits and captions, designing mobiles, weather charts, cartoons and animation, designing lettering and a presentation style for a series or special programme, making props such as charts, and even passports, foreign money, ration books, and other historical and period props. Graphic designers often regard themselves as experts in producing authentic material, as well as original designs. All designers are art-college trained, with degrees or diplomas in graphic designs. Most illustration work is carried out by freelance illustrators who are used on a regular basis, though some illustrators have been recruited in full-time posts to do both illustration and design.

Further information about career prospects, salaries, and other kinds of work undertaken by designers may be obtained from the BBC and Independent TV (see Useful addresses).

Technical graphic artists

Those who wish to enter more technical work may find employment in industrial companies, often allied to the engineering industry, and in other fields such as building, architecture, scientific and biological work, and in medical works. In the engineering field, the work may involve preparing drawings and plans from written specifications. This requires good interpretation skills in converting figures to two- and three-dimensional drawings in an accurate way. Work in these areas has been revolutionized by developments in computer illustration and computer-enhanced illustration.

Case Study

***Andy** works for a technical instrument company.*

Andy trained as a graphic designer but decided to enter the technical field. He works for a technical instrument company, mostly working on plans and drawings with research and development engineers who are designing new components. He also helps with training aids and produces some audio-visual material using computer design and photographic skills. He finds the job pays well and gives him the variety he needs. The level of accuracy and professionalism required in producing finished engineering drawings is to him the most challenging and satisfying part of the job. Some design consultancies may also employ technical graphic artists and illustrators.

Other areas of employment

Public relations departments in local authorities sometimes employ designers. Exhibition organizers and consultants employ interior, exhibition and graphic designers; many employ freelancers, often having a 'portfolio' of designers whom they can call upon for specific work. Printing firms may employ typographers and graphic designers.

Case Study

***Rob** is a designer/junior art director with a record company.*

'I got the job because the art director remembered me from a visit I had made eight months previous while still at college. I work with fairly strict budgets, and usually in close conjunction with the "artiste". Designs and artwork must be produced to package and promote the music produced (the product). This involves finding the right visual imagery to fit the music and the optimum method of producing the design decided upon, ie choosing and commissioning the illustrator or photographer where necessary. The actual design work I do myself wherever possible. There is a satisfaction in seeing a job through from initial concept to finished product and of course (it would be foolish to pretend otherwise) to find out other people's reactions to how successfully the recording is finally packaged. It is challenging to have to inform, advertise, help to make the product desirable, and yet still retain a closeness with the music and not affect the creditability of the performer.'

Some record companies will employ their own designers; others will use the services of freelance staff or advertising and publicity agencies. The music press and the *Music Yearbook* are helpful for ideas and addresses.

Illustrators

Illustrators emerging from specialist and graphic design courses may find full-time employment as designers or illustrators, but more often are commissioned by magazine and book publishers, design consultancies, advertising agencies and other employers on a freelance basis, sometimes through an artists' agent. Illustrators may also receive commissions by exhibiting work through galleries. In addition, scientific and technical illustrators may find freelance work, and sometimes full-time employment, in industry, medical and scientific publishers, research establishments, government departments, the National Health Service and in museums.

Staff at college, past students and established illustrators may be able to advise on practical issues, as will potential employers such as art directors with publishing companies and advertising agencies. The Association of Illustrators is the professional body.

It is concerned with all aspects of illustrating, provides advisory services and promotes illustrators' work. It also organizes an annual exhibition of illustrators, and publications include a regular newsletter and a Survival Kit which is particularly useful for the newly qualified illustrators. The kit covers all aspects of the work of the freelance illustrators, from setting up a studio and how to promote yourself, to what clients expect of illustrators, and useful reference sections on courses, printing jargon, and a list of artists' agents and their services.

Some illustrators apply for design jobs initially to gain some work experience and make contacts before taking on full-time freelance work; others may have already begun freelancing before leaving college and find that their work increases steadily from these initial contacts. The degree or diploma show at the end of the course brings many visitors to art and design departments, such as art directors from advertising agencies and publishing houses and artists' agents, all looking for new talent. Many illustrators find their first commissions in this way.

Making direct approaches to art directors with publishers, advertising agencies, design studios, television, or to artists' agents can be a daunting prospect. But art directors, on the whole, are keen to meet new college leavers and see their work. This involves assembling a portfolio of your work and fixing up visits by letter or telephone. This is the advice of one illustrator:

> Do your homework first. Find out what publications/type of books/publicity styles are produced by the organization you are approaching. Take a good selection of work – finished art work and working drawings, but not too much. Whoever you will see will have opinions about your work. Make sure you have your own opinions and don't be prepared to compromise on your work for the sake of getting a commission. If you're good enough, an art director somewhere will appreciate your style of work and be able to use you – if not then, possibly at a later date.

Sometimes, art directors may be able to advise you and recommend you to others – you need to be persistent in making contacts. One illustrator said she contacted 30 publishers in two months.

Artists' agents act on behalf of illustrators, finding them work with advertising agencies, publishing houses, and so on. Agents often charge a hefty commission (25 per cent upwards), but many illustrators use them, so you then don't have to spend valuable time looking for work.

Case Study

Marty *is a freelance illustator.*

Marty came through what she calls ' the usual school routine': O-Level Art, A-Level Art. She always wanted to draw so she enrolled on a one-year foundation course at Sheffield Polytechnic.

'It was a really fab start, opening my eyes to the range of options including fine art, sculpture, silversmithing and graphic design. If the college at Sheffield had done a graphics course I'd have stayed there to a BA, but they didn't so I had to choose where and what to do. I still wanted to draw, but didn't know what!

'My tutor asked what I enjoyed doodling and I said "people figures", so he suggested fashion design. Perplexing. Then we had a big meeting where we all had to say what course we'd chosen, so I decided fashion there and then, without actually looking into it at all.'

Marty studied BA Hons Fashion and Design at what was then Manchester Polytechnic. However, she was always keener on drawing and illustration so she managed to forge a successful career for herself as a fashion illustrator. After five years doing this she decided to work freelance, she had acquired good contacts for fashion illustration through her full-time work. But:

'I'd always wanted to do general illustration so I began a folio of more varied work. This still continues. Self-promotion is important; it's not only cheap but is also essential once you've established a working style, gained experience on magazines, etc ... It's important that your work is seen by art buyers. I take a page in an art annual each year, which is read by people I wouldn't get to see. It's time-consuming to organize to see every overworked art director in the industry, although it is good to do so in the early days when you're becoming established.

'Being reliable, professional, consistent and available to work are vital qualities. I found it necessary to build a relationship of trust with clients, who may become regulars now or in the future.

'When presenting yourself and your folio, all the common-sense rules apply, but I always kept a fairly small selection of art work – well edited, as I found that the art editors' time is precious too'.

'From the art annuals I was approached by artists' agents. I was wary for a while as I was getting enough work by myself. But it can be a mutually beneficial experience if you're willing to work with your agent to make progress and continue to self-promote. It changed the way I worked and saw my work.

'I get editorial or publishing work by having colour postcards printed of a recent piece of work and mailing them to magazines, etc ... My agent deals with advertising only. Fees for advertising work can be good but it's not regular: famine or feast! The backing of a good agent can be valuable but there are no guarantees of work, so I keep an eye on things I should be doing to generate work.

'Sometimes I feel I'll never get used to the ups and downs of freelance, but it's true that you get out what you put into work and I love illustrating!'

Case Study

***Jon** works as a freelance illustrator/photographer.*

Jon took a slightly different route into illustration from most artists: after leaving school with O- and A-Levels he completed a foundation course and went on to study graphic design at Central St Martin's; it was not until the beginning of his third year that he changed to specialize in illustration.

'I was advised to take an extra year to fully develop an illustrative style. This route has been an great advantage for me: studying graphics gave me a full understanding of the graphic design world from placements as an art director in an advertising agency and a design group. It also gave me a confidence and great love of typography.

'Central St Martin's prepared me extremely well for life as a professional illustrator; all the tutors were practising illustrators and we had regular projects with art directors.

'Some people got a lot of contacts from their degree show; I got one commission but the majority of my work came from interviews I organized with art directors. In my first year as a graduate I went on the Enterprise Allowance Scheme, which was invaluable for establishing my career, allowing me to concentrate on building a folio of commissioned work and not worrying about money.

'I have been working full-time as a freelance illustrator/photographer since graduating in 1989. I started by producing flat and sight relief collage illustrations and gradually moved into producing 3D illustrations and photography, then on to 5 x 4 transparencies. I still enjoy it greatly and have lots of ideas on how my work can develop.

'The last few years have been very busy. I have worked for a wide range of clients from magazines, design companies, advertising agencies to cable television. In 1994 I started advertising in the illustrators' book, *Contact*, the directory most widely used by art directors to commission work. It has brought in a lot of work. I was also approached by an agent who now represents me, although I still get work outside the agency.

'It is a profession that suits me really well as I have control of my work environment and to some extent decide when I work. It's extremely rewarding running your own business. I work from home, rather than a studio which I might find distracting. One week I'll be working on a magazine illustration, the next a brochure cover, the next an animated sequence.

'To be an illustrator you need to have a lot of get up and go and be able to pick yourself up from a knock back. You must have a lot of self-discipline, self-motivation and have good time management, along with the ability to get on with a wide range of people, and lots of enthusiasm.'

Jobs for history of art graduates

Graduates in the history of art and the history of design may enter further study and occupations related or unrelated to their degree subject.

- Postgraduate academic study or research in art history, design history, etc at universities. Some have followed study or training in other areas, such as administration, librarianship, secretarial work, the Works of Art courses at Sotheby's, and even in fine art or restoration – if students are sufficiently competent in the practice of art work. (A number of art history students continue with their art work while studying for their degree, although it may not be part of the course.)
- Teacher training – although few art history specialist teachers are employed in secondary education, it may be combined with other subjects or within general studies for the purposes of training and obtaining a teacher post later. There are few posts in further and higher education, many of which are more often taken up by those who have

completed a higher degree.

- History of art degrees may be relevant in occupations such as work in museums and art galleries; art administration; with art publishers as researchers, copy-writers, production assistants; restoration – if the practice of artwork is up to standard. They may also enter graduate occupations in industry, commerce, and local and central government.

Jobs in three-dimensional design

Three-dimensional design students from all subjects may go on to postgraduate study in a specialist area; jewellery, interior design, industrial design, furniture, ceramics, theatre design. Some may enter teacher training where there is a shortage of teachers in craft, design and technology skills, although students of three-dimensional subjects may also be found teaching visual arts subjects.

Many degree and vocational courses offer ceramics, furniture, jewellery, silversmithing, wood, metals, glass and plastics – where the design of functional or decorative objects may be the chief activity of the course. Some three dimensional design graduates may prefer to work as artists or craftspeople or designers, producing one-off objects in their own workshops, whereas others may apply their skills to more commercially oriented design, working on designs to be produced on a larger scale by manufacturing industry.

Jobs in industrial and product design.

Think of any gadget or piece of equipment you use in everyday life: a bicycle, a car, a refrigerator, kitchen equipment, furniture, heaters; or something in working life: a typewriter, office equipment, computer terminals, medical equipment. Somewhere along the line, an industrial or product designer will have contributed to the finished article. Nowadays, most industrial or product designers have completed courses in three-dimensional, product or industrial design, although graphics and textiles designers and fine artists have also been known to enter this field.

Industrial or product designers may be employed in design consultancies offering a range of design services to manufacturing and commercial companies, with in-house design groups in freelance building their own prototypes, with the aim of persuading a manufacturer to produce their designs on a commercial basis, or receive commissioned work. Some designers manufacture their own designs, where the production methods and equipment are on a small scale.

The work of the industrial designer has tremendous scope, but it should not be confused with that of the design engineer whose training will have been in engineering subjects and whose concern is in the design of the mechanical, electrical or electronic function, rather than the appearance. At a show of postgraduate designers' work at the Royal College of Art, there were designs for baby slings, desk top computer housing, vacuum flasks, watches, kitchen wear, seating and equipment for the handicapped – a 'hoverchair' and a Braille self-tutor. The contribution of the designer to our living and working environment is something that is increasingly being recognized and valued by manufacturers and consumers alike.

The Design Council promotes the work of British designers in all fields, especially in industrial and product design. It cultivates good relationships with manufacturers, maintains a register of recognized designers, displays work in its gallery in London, and publishes a monthly journal, *Design*, which features new work by designers. Similarly, the Chartered Society of Designers, the designers' professional organization, does much to improve standards of professionalism and promote the work of designers.

The work of the designer is concerned with the general aesthetic appearance of the product, but also takes into account the users' needs, and the manufacturing requirements. The designer may work closely with engineers and with production staff. Any small change in a design can mean changes in tooling-up for production. With strict budgets to work to, and possible production factors to take into account, the professional designer must consider the implications of his design work. At the end of the day, the product must look good, function well, and meet the users' needs. Some industrial design courses may include the study and application of engineering principles, whereas other three-dimensional design courses devote more time to 'creative' elements.

Case Study

***Mike** is a student of three-dimensional design working in the electrical industry, designing panels and 'cabinets' for cookers.*

'In my designs, it's no good making changes without consulting the design engineer. Moving knobs and switches about to give a more streamlined appearance may create havoc with the wiring, and the cooker may not function so well. I need to have a basic sympathy for engineering principles. I think taking a car to bits in my spare time while a student taught me a lot and gave me good grounding for this job! I begin my designs and scale drawings, including colour schemes, and then move on to set up mock-ups and models for the panels. The design is taken further when we build it into prototype later on. All along the way I am consulting with the design engineers and other staff.'

Case Study

***Sue** works as a design assistant for a pottery firm.*

Sue studied three-dimensional design with a product design bias, specialising in ceramics. She had some vacation work experience in the ceramics industry before graduating. Her first job is as a design assistant in the design studio of a pottery firm, and her work is confined to surface decoration of tableware. The first few months in her job were spent learning about the whole industrial process, seeing each manufacturing stage and learning something of the technical and chemical processes involved. At present she is working on a theme for a new range or tableware in the mid-price range, under the supervision of a senior designer.

Case Study

***Jane** specialized in furniture design, and since leaving college she has been employed as a designer with a company which markets office furniture and provides an office planning design service to their clients.*

'My work entails space-planning offices using office furniture provided by the companies we represent. This involves technical drawings, plans, elevations, visuals, drawing up quotes for furniture for client presentation. I may be involved in developing furniture products to meet changes in demand of customer and market. I supervise installations of furniture, coordinate warehouse and stock control. I also produce visuals or technical drawings for brochures and advertising material, together with audio-visual drawings. This is a small firm and, all in all, my work is very varied. The client liaison aspect is very important. As the work of the company develops, I hope I shall have opportunities for promotion. In my spare time I am studying for a diploma in Marketing with the intention of learning business procedure/strategy/managerial considerations and markets.'

Case Study

***Ellen** is an assistant goldsmith.*

'I was lucky to find this job. After leaving my industrial design course [silversmithing] I had several temporary jobs before coming across this one. At present, my final degree show work is displayed in the jeweller's shop window, which I hope will be good for my future as a designer! I was taken on because the shop was running behind with orders – we take individual commissions, remodelling, etc, the only shop in the area to do so, and despite great uncertainty in the trade it seems to be thriving. Now, having learned not to 'do everything backwards', I am trusted to do most of the simpler jobs and repairs that the menders won't do or have done wrong. It is most gratifying to find that you can do things, even if at first they are only very simple, to a very high standard and professional finish.'

Interior designers

Interior designers may join design practices – working with other interior designers and also with architects. Some may work in design practices and consultancies, offering a wider range of services alongside graphic designers, product designers, and textile designers. Other interior designers set up in freelance practice, though this is more likely after several years' experience in professional practice.

Interior designers may also join office furniture and design services, or work with in-house design groups, eg with furniture manufacturers, in the retail industry – providing bathroom and kitchen planning services to customers in the building companies, and in some industrial companies. The interior designer has an important contribution to make to our living and working environment. Most interior design work is for industry, shop interiors and displays, exhibitions, office interiors, hotels, businesses, airports, public buildings, and so on. Some interior designers may apply their design skills in other fields, such as theatre design, television set design, product design, and so on.

Theatre designers

Many students of theatre and design hope to find work in occupations related to their studies: in theatre, dance, opera, film, television, chiefly as set and costume designers, and sometimes in technical areas such as lighting, or in more administrative roles, for example, in stage management. Theatre designers may work on a freelance basis, or be employed full-time by national or provincial performing companies, and in film and television. It is the job of the theatre designer to work closely with producers, directors and actors to create the right setting and overall visual effect for a production, whether it is a historical drama or a modern dance performance. This involves times spent in researching for themes and ideas. A sympathy for the performed work, and for the way in which it is interpreted by the actors and directors, is vital. In larger companies, set and costume design may be carried out by separate specialists, although in smaller companies the designer may be responsible for the design of properties and costume.

A set designer may begin work for a production by preparing scale drawings and models of sets to suggest an overall theme, colour and style. The work will also include the selection of properties and supervising the making of some special properties, scene painting and the general construction of sets. The completion of the work requires the ability to see through the visual ideas into constructed full-size sets, often on limited budgets, and the supervision of craftspeople and scene painters. On leaving college, many newly qualified theatre designers begin work as assistants with small repertory companies, often in support roles, painting scenery, making costumes, or in community theatre. Others may be lucky to find design assistant posts with national theatre, opera and dance companies, or in film and television.

Case Study

***Roz** is a freelance theatre designer.*

Roz, a theatre graduate, works on a freelance basis and found she had enough contacts who would give her work, mostly with small theatre companies which often cannot afford to take on full-time design staff.

'When I'm in work I seem to work 24 hours a day designing, making costumes and scene painting. When I'm out of work, I try to find out more, read, walk, visit companies. I am gradually building up contacts and hope to become a specialist in design for dance.'

Case Study

***Di** is a milliner/jeweller with a large national theatre company.*

She wrote 'on spec' for the job and they asked her to come for interview. She works with one other colleague and it is their job to make all the hats for the main house shows.

'We work from designs and working drawings produced by senior designers. We are fortunate to work with leading international designers, from whom we learn a great deal. We also make a large amount of jewellery for production, often to our own design ideas, which I find very satisfying. During production we work lots of overtime, including weekends. Sometimes we can put our own designs into practice, after being given a rough idea of what is needed. My future plans are to find similar work with another large national company, maybe opera, to broaden my experience.'

---

5 Allied professions

Arts administrators

Arts administrators are professionals involved in the publicity, promotion and organization of artistic events of all kinds. Who are arts administrators? Where are they employed? What kind of work are they involved in?

Some arts administrators are graduates from arts disciplines such as fine art or art history but, equally, graduates from any subject – engineering, science, social studies and humanities – have entered this area of work. Most graduates will have had experience while at college, or after graduation, of organization performing or artistic activities and events, for example, voluntary work at a local arts centre, helping to set up an exhibition, helping to run a college arts festival, and organize drama productions. Other arts administrators may have had training or work experience in other fields after leaving school, having become involved in administration of the arts in their spare time, with amateur theatre groups, in festivals, etc.

So many different skills can be useful, even essential, in arts administration: accountancy, bookkeeping, publicity and public relations, journalism, typing, secretarial skills, catering management, and so on. A methodical and careful approach to organizational work is needed, along with creative flair and enthusiasm. An exhibition officer in an art gallery who once worked as a salesman for a textile company said: 'I hated the sales job, but please note, the training in basic admin was to stand me in good stead. Whatever you believe to the contrary, exhibitions need systems!'

Some, if not all, of the skills mentioned above may be required in any one job. In addition, interest in and knowledge of the art form with which you wish to work is expected. Some jobs may be specialist, ie information officer or publicity officer for an arts association or theatre, where experience of journalism and knowledge of publicity are an asset. An assistant in a small gallery, on the other hand, said of her job:

> There's just me and the gallery owner. I do everything from making tea to fending off the creditors. I'm responsible for all bookings, arranging transport for art works, all the paperwork involved, sales, hanging works, invigilating in the gallery, doing the accounts, cleaning, visiting some of the artists on our books, and on occasion I have been known to do the gallery owner's shopping when he is busy. I would certainly not describe my job as routine or boring!

One vital point: the arts administrator must have an understanding of the needs of creative artists, whether actors, dancers, visual artists or musicians. It is not a job for the frustrated artist or performer seeking to satisfy his or her own creative needs, although a creative approach is needed to help create the right atmosphere, initiate the right kind of events and satisfy the needs of the artist or performer and those who come to see the performances and exhibitions.

Where do arts administrators work?

- *The Arts Council.* Its chief role is to administer government aid to the arts, and there are relatively few jobs at their headquarters. The Officers in Literature, Music, Drama and Visual Arts have experience and qualifications in their own specialized fields. There are a few assistant administrative and secretarial positions for which competition is fierce.
- *The Crafts Council* performs a similar function to the Arts Council, but this is directed to promoting and providing finance for the crafts, such as jewellery, ceramics, glass, weaving, and so on.

- *Regional Arts Boards* perform a similar function to the Arts Council, but at a regional level (see Useful addresses) administering funding for the arts and for the crafts council, organizing publicity of the arts, liaising with local authorities, supporting and promoting artists, performers and craftspeople in the area. There are posts as drama officers, crafts officers, community arts officers. These involve committee work, receiving grant applications, liaising with local societies, arts groups, and sometimes colleges. There may also be public relations and publicity posts, administrative assistant and secretarial jobs.
- *Arts centres, theatres, ballet, opera, concert halls.* Here posts exist in stage management, front-of-house management, publicity, accounts, and so on. As well as managing and organizing programmes of events, administrators meet the needs of resident and visiting companies, and there is often the general maintenance and care of the building to consider, bars, catering, general office work, and so on. Community theatre groups, touring companies and the orchestra may also employ arts administrators.
- *Community Arts.* There is a role for those with administrative skills to work in this field, on a permanent, part-time or voluntary basis.
- *Art and craft galleries and shops.* Opportunities may exist in national and provincial galleries for exhibition organizers and publicity officers, and administrators in private galleries. Some galleries run by universities employ full-time or part-time exhibition staff.
- *Artists' personal assistant.* A handful of artists employ personal assistants or general dogsbodies to do the accounts, answer the phone, arrange exhibitions, pack up art works for travelling, and generally organize things in order to leave the artists free to pursue their work.
- *Arts festivals.* Many cities and towns throughout the country have annual festivals of art events, performances and exhibitions. Some of the larger festivals employ full-time or part-time staff, and extra casual staff may be taken on when the time of the festival draws near. The Arts Council pub-

lishes a list of festivals and their dates each year which may be obtained from Dillons Arts Bookshop in Covent Garden, London.

- *Local authorities* run museums and art galleries, leisure and amenity centres, conference centres, recreation and sports complexes where there may be careers in municipal entertainment, recreation and leisure management. In addition, some local authorities employ arts officers who liaise with Regional Arts Boards and art societies in the locality.
- *Private galleries*. There are many privately owned and run galleries in most major cities, dealing with a portfolio of artists for whom they sell and organize exhibitions, publicity, etc. The famous area in London for private galleries is Cork Street, overspilling into New Bond Street and around Burlington Arcade, though numerous others exist. You may wish to target a gallery that handles a favourite artist's work, or a school of work, of which you are knowledgeable or interested in.

Case Study

***Peter** is the technical manager of a London gallery.*

'In total I spent seven years at art college, the first year being a vigorous and varied art and design foundation course at Derby. By the end of this, I'd decided on the direction of fine art.

'I took a break for a couple of years to work and gain commercial experience. I spent one year at a design company specializing in corporate identity and packaging and the second year doing voluntary work at two art galleries.

'I embarked next on a four-year Fine Arts course at Newcastle which I found fairly ideal, being suited to the type of student who was very highly motivated. This was succeeded by two years on an MA Fine Arts course at Reading, which was good, being so opposite in approach to Newcastle. I felt as though I had the benefit of two very different philosophies. It was during these two years that I started working part-time at a commercial art gallery in London, as I was commuting from there to Reading at any time. I can definitely say that, in retrospect, the voluntary work first started four to five years before was invaluable in getting this work.

'I am working there full-time now as a technical manager, working on all transport and shipping administration, as well as sorting out the problems that occur on installing each new show. The job is constantly busy and often very stressful and demanding, requiring a careful balance between office and practical work. I enjoy the varied mix of tasks and the fact that new challenges arise constantly. One shouldn't enter this field with the expectation of great pay: the best rewards lie in working alongside the artists, promoting their work and understanding the structure behind a commercial fine art operation.'

Training

For those thinking of entering arts administration, the advice generally given is to get some experience first, and it may be important to gain some extra skills and put these into practice before looking for your first job. It is useful, anyhow, to test out your commitment to this type of work, so that you are better equipped and have more to offer when applying for your first job. Secretarial skills and training are very useful. Many arts administrators have begun their careers with a secretarial post in an arts organization. Others may do box-office work, be assistant stage managers, administrative assistant, and so on. There are two full-time courses of professional training in arts administration, run in conjunction with the Arts Council, at the City University's Centre for Arts. Both are postgraduate or post-experience courses; therefore applicants have normally already had some related work experience. Some arts administrators may work for professional qualifications in the field of museums and art galleries, public relations, public administration, recreation management, management studies, accountancy, and so on.

Career prospects

Vacancies in arts administration attract large numbers of applications. Salaries, especially at the beginning, are not high, but the infinite variety, the scope for developing individual jobs and the special satisfaction achieved, make arts administration an exciting field in which to work.

Finding a job

The Creative and Media Appointments pages of *The Guardian* and other periodicals and newspapers listed in Chapter 9 are the main sources of vacancies. Some entrants to arts administration may be offered a full-time job as a result of doing voluntary work in the same arts organization. Speculative applications to arts organizations may well result in an interview.

Art therapists

Art therapy is still a relatively new profession, and is allied to other remedial therapies, occupational, music and drama therapy. Art therapy has a role to play as a healing aid in improving the condition and often the quality of life for hospital patients or people with terminal or long-term illnesses, those in psychiatric care, the mentally and physically handicapped, and those receiving remedial tuition in schools. Art therapy may be used as an interpretational aid. For example, psychiatric patients may find it easier to express feelings and emotions visually through painting or working with clay and wood, rather than verbally. Art therapists work alongside psychiatrists and psychotherapists and encourage patients to express themselves. As well as being good teachers and facilitators, art therapists must therefore have an understanding of psychopathology, which is studied as part of art therapy training. In addition to finding employment in hospitals, art therapists work in special schools for people with mental and learning difficulties as art teachers, using art in a number of ways – as a means of communication, in assessment, and as a way of encouraging creativity. They may also be employed as craft instructors in social services day centres for the mentally and physically handicapped.

Entry qualifications and training

Most entrants to art therapy are graduates, usually in art and design subjects, and occasionally in other subjects such as education, sociology or psychology where there is also evidence of artistic ability. In order to qualify as an art therapist there are courses of professional training which may be entered by graduates usually after some relevant experience (see Chapter 3).

There are a number of ways in which experience may be gained. Some people may do voluntary work in hospitals or day centres while still at college. One graduate gained some art therapy experience by writing to her local hospital enquiring about posts. She was offered a job as an art therapist which she did for one year. 'There is a great deal of job satisfaction – loads of responsibility to the patients, many tasks involved – creative activities, office work, liaising between school kids, social workers, psychotherapists, doctors and nurses. There's scope for ingenuity, but little of my own creativity at present.' She is now doing a one-year teacher training course. Nursing experience is also a useful way of gaining insight into the work and working environment.

Another route to art therapy is after teacher training and a period of teaching experience in art subjects in ordinary schools, when the teacher's interests may incline towards more remedial and specialist work. This may then be followed by an art therapy course. It is also possible to combine a postgraduate teacher-training course with art therapy training. One or two such courses exist.

Here are some comments from a fine art graduate:

> I am doing a PGCE in Art Education and Art Therapy, which I entered in the September after leaving my first degree course in fine art. I will become a qualified graduate teacher and a registered therapist. I do not wish to pursue teaching. On the course I have held placements in a children's hospital (as teacher), an inner city multiracial comprehensive school, two adult psychiatric hospitals (as art therapist), and as an adolescent assessment centre (as art therapist and teacher).
>
> The course lectures include psychotherapy, psychiatry, psychology, sociology, education and philosophy. The course is geared towards group psychotherapy workshops – towards a fuller awareness and understanding of oneself. I find the work very satisfying and creative, and I like the variety. The psychiatric experience has been very useful, especially in psychiatric hospitals where I have worked

> as an art therapist. After the course finishes I have been accepted for a post as trainee social worker. In the future I hope to return to art therapy in psychiatric hospitals part-time.

Obtaining a further job, particularly one which is well paid, can often prove difficult. A recently trained therapist was offered a job as an occupational therapy aide but instead took a post as a teacher in a special school, where she was able to earn £2500 pa more. Pay varies considerably throughout art therapy, mainly because of the variety of employers: the Health Service, education, social service departments, etc, although some attempts are being made by the profession to standardize salary scales. However, the personal rewards and satisfaction in this field of work can be enormous, as they are with many therapeutic professions. If you would like to find out more about art therapy, try to arrange a visit to an art therapist at your local hospital or in a special school.

Community artists

For years, many artists and performers have taken active roles in their own communities and encouraged other people to express themselves through artistic means – by teaching, community work, adult education classes, and so on. In recent years, some of these artists and performers have established a new identity, calling themselves community artists.

At the start, most community artists were unpaid. They worked with local community groups in a variety of ways: setting up a community newspaper; helping local residents create their own play or music; working on creative projects with play schemes. The artist or performer became a *facilitator*, an *organizer*, a *teacher of skills* to people who wished to express themselves and their ideas through participating in theatre, music, dance, the visual arts, video, film, radio, crafts, photography, puppetry. The number of community arts projects in the UK has grown from around 100 to over 1000, with groups or individuals operating on a regular basis. Many of these now receive regular support and some finance from Regional Arts Boards or direct from the Community Arts panel of the Arts Council of Great Britain, from local authorities or charities, though with present public expenditure cuts the future of many projects may be uncertain. Here are some examples of the ways in which community artists work and the projects they may set up or become involved with:

- a community arts centre with its own premises, often in inner cities, may have been set up by volunteers to provide premises for play activities for children, or a community centre for social activities. Once established, permanent and salaried posts may be created. Workers and volunteers may help run community festivals; arts/crafts classes; theatre groups; dance; provide printing facilities for local clubs or pressure groups to print their own posters, etc often with the support of social services departments.
- Some work in summer play schemes or adventure playgrounds.
- Some local authorities and new town development corporations employ community artists for community development work – helping to bring residents together; running leisure activities; teaching arts and crafts skills.
- Some town artists work with planners and architects in planning the living environment in new towns.
- Regional Arts Boards may employ community arts workers in conjunction with the local authority to initiate projects in a given area.

Career structure and pay

Community artists have some kind of creative skill to contribute and many are all-round performing artists who have had art college or drama school training. Little formal training exists, though there are some art and design and performance courses with a social or community element. There are no rigid career structures or entry requirements and financial reward and high salaries are not a regular feature. Few full-time salaried posts exist – those that do are with longer-established well-funded projects.

On the whole, many community artists find it difficult to see their own work as a long-term career. Hours are irregular; community arts activities take place in their spare time.

Related areas of work are theatre design, arts administration, art and design.

Entering community arts work

Involvement in community arts while a student or after college can have many benefits for the student (and for the community) despite the lack of career structure and scarcity of full-time jobs in this field of work. Many students become involved in projects and summer play schemes on a voluntary basis while still at college. Community arts can be a way of testing out skills and developing confidence in a wide range of roles and activities, before deciding on a career direction. In the past, those who have worked with community arts groups have moved into youth and community work, teaching, social work, arts administration, and some have become professional community artists. Your Regional Arts Board can put you in touch with community artists in your area.

Case Study

Helen *is a fine art graduate working in community arts.*

'I left college, knowing I wanted to work in a community arts centre in my home town. I had worked there in college holidays, and they needed helpers so I began work on a voluntary basis. After four months the centre received a grant from the Regional Arts Board and funding from the local authorities for one year. Two full-time posts were advertised and I was lucky enough to get one of them, as I had (I hope) proved my worth during the time I had been there.

'There are four of us all together, two of us working part-time on a voluntary basis. We are a musician/photographer, a drama specialist, a graphic designer, and my speciality is mural painting. I also do puppetry and mime. I must immodestly say that our talents do not stop there. We all have to muck in and do everything from building renovation to general organization and admin. All our activities are decided jointly by the committee of the community centre, of which two of us are members.

'This year we have helped to run a fund-raising bonfire night festival; an old folks' entertainment evening (for which I helped local kids build a puppet theatre and run a show); regular classes in photography, drama/mime, silk-screen printing; mothers-and-toddlers meetings; painting a mural at a local school involving all the kids; summer play schemes; activity afternoons at the centre for handicapped kids. We don't set out to impose our ideas on people, but we can teach skills so that they can interpret things in their own way.

'I live two minutes away from the centre, so I always seem to be on call, which is OK, but I don't have time for a private life. The community centre is my life, I suppose, and I don't feel like moving because the work is so satisfying and varied, though the pay is not so good. My future plans are uncertain, though I am becoming increasingly interested in working with the handicapped.'

Jobs in conservation and restoration

The preservation and repair of works of art and other objects of value are carried out chiefly in national and provincial museums and art galleries; by a smaller number of commercial restoration firms; in some craft workshops; and by some conservators working with private collections or independent museums. Objects receiving the attention of conservators and restorers include works of art – oil paintings, sculptures, prints, drawings, etc; natural history exhibits; and archaeological remains.

Conservation and restoration is a very specialized field, employing a small number of highly skilled people who have normally undergone a lengthy training in order to meet the level of knowledge and standards of workmanship required.

The Crafts Council Conservation Unit (see Useful addresses) maintains a register of conservators and restorers, provides information about training in conservation and carries out research into activities central to a well-founded national conservation service.

What skills and qualities are required?

Those involved in conservation and restoration usually specialize in this area of work and may be concerned with the practical care, cleaning, preservation and repair of objects. A detailed understanding of the objects, the materials with which they are made and their history, is needed. In preserving objects it is important not to let the artistic skill of the restorer influence the appearance of the work in any way – respecting the original intentions of the creator. Conservators and restorers may also be involved in valuing and classifying pieces, working alongside art historians and archaeologists. Some restoration can take years of careful work.

Entry qualifications, training and courses

Those entering conservation and restoration do so from a variety of backgrounds:

- graduates and those with equivalent professional qualifications in the physical and natural sciences, art and design, art history, archaeology
- trainee craftspeople in specialized fields, such as stone, plasterwork, gilding, furniture, etc can train to be restorers, and those with basic craft skills may be employed as technical assistants in museum conservation departments.

Increasingly, a scientific background is important – the Museums Association (see Useful addresses) recommends a minimum of two A-levels, of which one should be chemistry. A knowledge of chemistry or physics may be vital in understanding the composition of objects, in cleaning and restoration. Conservators may also have to enlist the help of scientists with X-ray techniques and chemical analysis, in order to understand further the objects with which they are working. In conservation work you will find art and design graduates with an understanding of science, or at least a willingness to gain a working knowledge of this area while training and, equally, science graduates with practical and artistic skills. Some entrants to conservation work may have already completed voluntary work with a local conservation society or museum.

In addition to the desired qualities and qualifications listed above, most people entering conservation work will undergo a period of training. A selection of courses in conservation and restoration at colleges in the UK is given in Chapter 3. These can last from one to four years, and subjects and specialisms offered range from easel painting to clocks. The courses include practical work, historical studies and, in most cases, science subjects as applied to conservation work. On completion of these courses, applicants may try for officer conservation posts in museums and art galleries, and with private concerns. Some of the courses have grants available in the form of bursaries or studentships, or students may rely on discretionary grants from their local authority. The course to which you apply will tell you where you should apply for financial support.

Trainee positions

The national galleries and museums, such as the British Museum and Area Museum Councils that govern museums and galleries in other parts of the UK, advertise trainee posts where those with the basic qualifications receive practical and academic training in conservation on the job. As with all vacancies in conservation work, only a few trainee posts appear each year. Trainees usually receive close supervision by experienced conservators and restorers in their practical work, and are encouraged to follow academic study, visit other conservation areas, and work towards the Museums Diploma of the Museum's Association or Diploma in Conservation, which can take several years. Applications to full conservation officer posts may be made after gaining experience and museum qualifications.

One example of a training scheme is that run by the Victoria and Albert Museum which lasts two or three years full-time. Candidates require a relevant degree. It leads to the Diploma in Conservation of the Victoria and Albert Museum and of the Royal Academy of Art. Information is obtained from the Royal College of Art (see Useful addresses).

Other commercial firms may give you practical experience, but there are no formal schemes to ensure that you will receive adequate training. In addition to gaining practical experience, some short and part-time courses are available in colleges and may be run by organizations such as the Rural Development Commission (see Useful addresses).

Job vacancies

Few vacancies appear with the major employers in museums and art galleries, and opportunities with small conservation work shops and commercial restorers are limited. Training can take from two to five years on top of a degree or other relevant qualifications, and once trained, promotion from conservation officer to senior positions in museums can take some time as there is little movement from post to post in the profession, the work being so specialized. Salary scales can be supplied by the Museums Association and all the posts are advertised in the *Museum Bulletin*. Other relevant journals and sources of vacancies are listed later in this book. As with many artistic and creative professions, personal rewards and satisfaction are considerable.

Case Study

***Anna** is a fine art student who obtained a post as assistant conservation officer (ACO)(a training position) at a national museum.*

While at college and after graduation, she spent several periods doing voluntary work in museums, experiences on which she was able to draw when making applications for jobs later. In addition to her post, she has carried on with her own drawing and painting, has attended pottery evening classes, and is also a member of the City of London Archaeological Society which organizes lectures and digs. She says:

'ACO is a training position, so the work involves about 70 per cent practical work with organic material cleaning, consolidating and repairing objects and textiles, at first under the supervision of a senior, and now repeatedly making my own judgements about treatments etc. Thirty per cent of the time is taken up with lectures on chemistry and techniques. The work is satisfying and the results are usually very rewarding. The responsibility of deciding how to treat valuable objects can be nerve-racking, although advice is always available. The continual learning of techniques and culture is very stimulating. However, I should like more experience with metals or ceramics, or conservation on digs. Pay is adequate but not very good. Promotion is likely after four or five years. My future plans are to remain in this job and to take examinations for the Diploma in Conservation for the Museums Association.'

She adds that any kind of experience is very important when entering careers in museums.

Jobs in museums and art galleries

There are many different posts in public museums and galleries, and for some, an art and design, or art history qualification is useful, if not essential. Vacancies do not appear frequently and when they do there is often fierce competition.

National museums are funded from central government and are mostly centred in London, for example, the Victoria and Albert Museum, the British Museum, and the National Gallery. Provincial museums and galleries are run and financed by local authorities. These vary in size from quite large metropolitan or county museums and gallery collections to small galleries and museums which may be attached to public libraries. In addition, many specialist collections exist, such as museums of industrial archaeology, rural life, costume, or crafts. *Museums and Art Galleries in Great Britain*, a directory published by the Museums Association (see Useful addresses), gives a comprehensive guide to the collections and the museums and galleries in which they are housed. Private galleries and museums and commercial arts galleries also employ administrative and curatorial staff.

Entry qualifications and training

For most of the posts mentioned below, degrees or professional qualifications are normally required. Most museums will expect evidence of a commitment to museum work from applicants, many of whom will have had some experience through voluntary work while at college or after graduation. Many museums are willing to take voluntary workers for short periods. Voluntary experience in museums is also organized by the National Association of Decorative and Fine Arts Societies (NADFAS) (see Useful addresses) and there are many amateur archaeological and conservation societies which may provide similar experience. Alternatively, depending on the type of post applied for, some experience in another field, such as arts administration or design experience, may be desirable.

Professional full-time postgraduate courses in museum and art gallery studies prepare graduates for entry to museum work. Once employed in a museum or art gallery, you are encouraged to work for the Museums Diploma of the Museums Association. Training for museum work is described in more detail in the publications listed in further reading.

Work in museums and art galleries for which an art and design or art history qualification is useful or essential

- Careers in *conservation and restoration* are discussed separately.
- *Assistant keeper, keepers and other curatorial staff* are responsible for the acquisition, exhibition and explanation of collections. Where art, design or craft collections are concerned, keepers may have degrees in art history, or in art and design with a high academic content. These posts combine academic with administrative work, and applicants would need a special knowledge or at least interest in the collection with which they will be working.
- *Museum assistant.* This job may vary in content, from carrying out basic routine maintenance and classification work to responsibility for the art of a collection, rather like the work of the keeper. It is a trainee position, while you work for the professional diploma of the Museums Association. Some museum assistants may have degrees or equivalent qualifications; others may be recruited with GCSEs and A-Levels. Art history and art and design qualifications are relevant for posts with collections in the arts, design and crafts areas.
- *Education officers* are concerned with education within and outside the museum, and in its relationship with schools and publications, organization of holiday activities for chil-

dren in connection with the museum, adult education, lectures, special touring exhibitions for schools and colleges, and so on. Most education staff have teaching qualifications and several years' teaching experience, together with a degree relevant to museum work, or at least a proven strong interest in the work of museums. Art and design graduates with teaching experience may move into this field of work.

- *Designers* mostly work in larger museums which may have a design department, employing three-dimensional designers, model-makers, graphic designers and display staff. In small museums, one person may have to carry out all of these tasks – thus needing a wide range of skills. Art and design qualifications are necessary, and most applicants will have had previous design experience.
- *Exhibition staff.* Larger museums may employ specialists to organize and mount exhibitions. With an art gallery, this can involve all the administrative tasks to do with mounting an exhibition of an artist's work, for example, contacting owners of works, organizing publicity, working with design staff in setting up the exhibition. Some exhibition staff may be involved in education activities, such as organizing lectures. Many staff in this area have art history, or art and design qualifications and proven experience in arts administration, while others may come from graphics, interior design or even architectural backgrounds.
- *Research assistants* may be employed by national museums to carry out specialist academic research in connection with a certain collection. This may involve some routine tasks, such as classification, and cataloguing and literature search. With arts collections, art history degrees or art and design degrees with considerable academic content are normally required.
- *Technical staff.* Those with practical skills, such as carpentry or joinery, may be employed to support the work of museums staff. Only the larger museums may employ photographers whose work is mainly to do with recording specimens and scientific work. Photographers may be used on

a freelance basis by other museums.

- *Other types of work.* A very few museums and galleries employ specialists to carry out public relations or publicity work, for which experience in publicity or journalism may be useful. Sometimes administrative staff may be recruited to run museum shops, handling printing or materials, or sales work.
- *Related employers.* Charities, such as the National Trust, private collections and stately homes, may all employ staff for work similar to that carried out in museums, but job opportunities are normally very limited. Commercial art galleries employ staff for administrative, publicity and sales work, and their addresses may be found in the Arts Review Yearbook and Directory (see Further reading).

Job vacancies and career prospects

Most of the kinds of post mentioned above are advertised in the *Museums Bulletins*, the monthly journal of the Museums Association, and in other publications. Local authorities are responsible for advertising posts in most provincial museums. It is important to note that the content of jobs with similar titles may vary from museum to museum and that the job advertisements and descriptions should be read carefully before applying. Public expenditure cuts have affected the number of posts in museums and galleries in the UK. Competition for posts is considerable, and promotion to senior positions may take up to five years or more.

Designers in television and films

There are numerous occupations in the film, television and photography industries, most requiring engineering, technical or scientific expertise and qualifications, and it is in these technical areas that most of the opportunities lie; opportunities in more creative areas are popular and extremely competitive.

The major television companies, BBC and ITV, and the regional networks employ limited numbers of designers in several different fields. Vacancies rarely arise but speculative applications may be worth while. Work more frequently comes via individual programme-making companies, as more and more programmes are bought in. Film companies also employ designers, some of whom come from the theatre, television or from a relevant art and design course.

Related work is photography, film making and medical photography.

Jobs in television or films

- *Set design.* Designers for television and film are responsible for creating the right production, in close consultation with the producer and director. This may involve creating scenery and selecting furnishings and props. In television, complex theatrical scenery may be required for a drama production, simple screens and studio furniture for current affairs programmes. Most designers and design assistants come from the theatre, or courses in theatre design, interior design, architecture, exhibition design, three-dimensional design and even landscape architecture. Creativity and an ability to represent proposed work in two-dimensional and architectural drawings are required. Special skills, such as model-making, are sometimes sought. Scenic artists work with designers in painting scenery and backcloths which require the ability to paint on a large scale, often working under pressure. Fine artists, painters and sculptors may find opportunities in this area.
- *Costume design.* Includes the maintenance and cataloguing of costume, the occasional exhibition, designing and building costumes for historical drama, and so on. Fashion design or theatre design graduates may be employed, or those already with experience in the theatre. Much of the support work is carried out by machinists from the clothing industry.
- *Graphic design.* See Chapter 4.
- *Film making and film animation.* Graphic designers and illustrators may find work as designers and animation special-

ists with film companies. There are some companies and studios specializing in animation work. There are one or two art and design courses specializing in animation for film and TV. See Michael Selby, *Careers in Television and Radio* (in Further reading).

Teaching

For many years, teaching seemed an obvious choice of career for the art school-leaver; it promised continued involvement with artwork; the necessary one-year training course was fairly accessible; and it was reasonably easy to find a teaching post. Now the situation has changed. In recent years there has been a dramatic decline in the number of teaching posts, owing to education expenditure cuts and the expected fall in rolls with the lower national birth rate, and it is no longer possible to be sure of a post after training.

Despite increases in student numbers, education cuts have also affected the number of posts in higher education, particularly posts in art schools, and art and design departments of colleges and universities. Practising artists, designers and artist-craftspeople have in the past relied on part-time teaching for a regular income and contact with colleges, but in schools particularly, those now entering teaching have to think more seriously about their commitment to the profession, knowing that there is no certainty of a job. Teaching has become an all-graduate profession. At whatever level you choose to teach, the possession of a degree is now a basic requirement, as is the possession of GCSE level English and Mathematics.

Secondary schools and further education

What subjects are offered in art and design departments? Painting, sculpture, drawing, printmaking, graphics; increasingly, three-dimensional subjects: ceramics, wood, metal; textiles; and in some schools video and photography.

The design and craft area is one of the teaching areas in which there are often unfilled posts. In recent years it has been generally recognized that a design sense, aesthetic appreciation, and the development of skills required in designing and making things, are as vital a part of education as the study of other academic and practical subjects. Many schools now have design departments which may combine what was technical studies and handicrafts, the emphasis being on learning through the use of materials. Design studies can include creative metalwork, ceramics, woods, plastics, furniture, textiles, technical drawing and, in some schools, product design and engineering. The spectrum of qualifications held by teachers in this area ranges from qualified artists and designers to those with technical and engineering qualifications and experience. Students of three-dimensional and other design areas may find they have a contribution to make to craft, design and technology teaching.

Art and design teachers in secondary schools normally hold either a degree in art and design, plus a one-year postgraduate art teacher qualification (ATC/ATD); or a postgraduate certificate of education (PGCE); or a BEd or BEd Hons degree with art and design as a major subject. Leavers from vocational art and design courses may have to complete a full BEd degree in order to enter the teaching profession. However, some ATC/ATD courses are prepared to consider applicants with art and qualifications other than degrees, and some applicants could also be eligible for shortened BEd courses.

Primary schools

This area of teaching has suffered the worst cutbacks, and few posts are available. However, teachers in primary schools offer general subjects and have been specially trained for this age range.

Posts are held by BEds who have specialized in primary education, and graduates in art and design and in other subjects may enter primary teaching after one-year postgraduate certificate in education (PGCE), having specialized in the primary age groups. The English and Maths GCSE requirement mentioned above also applies to primary teaching.

Higher education

Teachers and lecturers in art and design may be involved with foundation, vocational or degree courses. New college-leavers are less likely to be considered for posts in higher education without postgraduate study or after some years' design experience, but it does happen. Artists and designers who have in some way made a mark for themselves through successes in their area, resulting in publicity, may find they are invited to colleges to offer fresh, young inspiration and input to a particular project or even to a course. Part-time teaching combines well with a freelance career but, as has already been pointed out, few posts of this kind are now available. A teaching qualification, however, is not essential and once some expertise is gained you can begin to circulate your CV to be put on record, should your particular specialisms and experience be required.

Adult education

In compiling this book, information was received from several art college-leavers who had obtained part-time teaching in adult education. Some had completed one-year teacher-training courses after their degrees, and were unable to find full-time teaching posts in schools, or had chosen to teach adults. Others may be able to teach adult education classes without a teaching qualification. There are adult education centres in most towns and cities in the UK, and although adult education budgets have been subject to cuts, many classes exist in a range of subjects. Some classes may be self-financing, thus not having to rely on local education authority support.

How does one find employment in adult education? Sometimes a post may be advertised or it may simply be a question of contacting an adult education centre to see if they are short of tutors, giving some idea of what you can offer, or possibly designing a course which you are prepared to teach, and offer your services in this way. For example, a textile graduate, working as a freelance designer, offered a ten-unit course at her local adult education centre (one 2-hour evening session per week) for which she was paid per session. The course was designing and making children's clothes. The centre was keen and had the facilities available, and the classes proved to be extremely popular.

The adult education centre may be able to help you cost out a course by furnishing you with average costs of courses, how much people are prepared to pay, what fees staff received, abilities and levels of skill, etc. You could make an appointment to see the head or deputy to discuss preliminary ideas.

The names and addresses of adult education centres may be obtained from your local library. In addition, the WEA community centres, community arts centres, youth clubs and so on may well be pleased to invite you to run classes on their premises maybe during the summer when premises and facilities would otherwise be unused.

Special education

Teaching in schools for the physically and mentally handicapped normally requires a degree and teaching qualifications and several years' experience in teaching normal children. Art therapy training is also relevant (see Chapter 5).

The general entry requirements for teacher-training courses, grants, and the methods of application are fully described in Chapter 3.

Some questions you may have about training

What is a PGCE art and design? The postgraduate art teachers' certificate or diploma is a one-year course for art and design graduates intending to specialize in teaching art or design subjects chiefly in secondary schools. These courses combine study in education and teaching methods with periods of teaching practice in schools. In addition, some courses may offer special options in remedial teaching, further or adult education, art therapy and certain other special areas. Courses are offered at centres all over the UK.

Art and design graduates opting to teach in primary schools or wishing to train for general subject teaching, possibly to middle school level, will find a PGCE (primary education) more suited to their needs than an art and design PGCE which is for specialist secondary school art teaching. In craft, design and technology (CDT) teaching, a PGCE is a relevant qualification, but some specialized PGCE courses exist in CDT teaching. It is important that you explore the differences between different PGCE courses for yourself so that you find the one most suited to your needs.

What can you do to prepare yourself for a teaching career? It is considered an advantage to have other experience before entering teacher training, as mature entrants are often thought to have a greater commitment to the profession after other kinds of work. In order to test your motivation, involvement with young people – in community arts activities, summer play schemes, youth clubs, or adventure playgrounds – during or after college, is helpful, and good experience to have on your application form when later applying for jobs. Sometimes it is possible and even desirable to spend a short period observing or helping in a school. Contact your old school, or your local education authority, or the teacher training college to which you may eventually apply and they may be able to arrange for you to visit a school.

Career prospects and applying for jobs

As has already been stated, teaching posts are in short supply, but if you are persistent, are prepared to be flexible geographically and in the range of subjects you can offer in art and design, you may well find a post. Additional skills such as photography, video, a willingness to help with games, clubs and societies, will certainly help your application. Promotion prospects have been affected by education cuts. However, if you are able to offer suitable skills in crafts, design and technology (CDT) this is a good area to consider.

The periodicals and journals in which teaching posts appear are listed in Further reading. It is also possible to obtain vacancy lists from individual local education authorities, and sometimes speculative applications to colleges and adult education centres may be fruitful. For independent schools, the Incorporated

Association of Preparatory Schools and the Independent Schools Information Service (see Useful addresses), may be able to help with further information on how to obtain a post although posts are advertised in the main teaching journals.

Case Study

***Frances** is a sculpture and painting student, who completed an ATC and now teaches in a large comprehensive school.*

'I teach in an art department of five. The other teachers do general art teaching and offer specialisms in sculpture, pottery and printmaking. I offer painting, sculpture and also do some remedial work. I have my own tutor group in the lower part of the school, 11 – 12 year olds. I teach the 11 – 14 age group mostly, but do some exam and sixth-form work with older children. I prefer teaching the lower age group – they seem to be so much more imaginative and free from inhibitions than the older children. I think exams can spoil enjoyment and curb creativity in art.

'A typical lesson might be on a theme. Last week with the third years, we talked about food and looked at lots of pictures to do with the way food is depicted. The contrast in the way food is shared out between starving and well-fed people in the world was brought out by the children. They started to paint and one group decided to work on a large collage to be continued this week. Another lesson might be more technical – drawing the school buildings, to look at the use of perspective. I try to run my lessons so that after I introduce a theme, the class generates the ideas and decides on the direction the lesson should take.

'I know some art teachers find teaching draining, and they stop doing their own work. It can be tiring. There are so many constraints in the way the school day is organized and in the materials we have available. I get a lot of stimulus from the kids, though, and I am illustrating children's stories in my spare time, and working on my own sculpture in clay at home.'

Related work is art therapy, community arts, education officer in museums or arts and craft instructors. Some adult training centres for the mentally and physically handicapped may employ art and design graduates with, and sometimes without, teaching qualifications. Posts may be advertised in the educational press.

If you want to teach overseas, unless you speak the language of the country in which you wish to teach, getting a post can be difficult. You could do a TEFL course (teaching English as a foreign language) and combine your art/creative teaching with teaching English. Contact the British Council for advice and information (see Useful addresses).

Getting started

Top Tips

- You could always avoid it! Extend your college life by up to three years by doing a postgraduate course – get the opportunity and facilities to carry on your work.
- There are various enterprise schemes which offer a weekly income and often back-up support, but expect to have at least £1000 of your money to invest in your own business. For instance the Graduate Enterprise Programme, the Design Enterprise Programme, the London Enterprise Agency, the Business Start-up Scheme and the Crafts Council Setting Up Scheme (see Useful addresses).
- If you are a fine artist or performance artist you could apply for a grant from the Arts Council or the Regional Arts Board, or the Prince's Trust, (see Useful addresses).
- Network, if you are looking for a job, use all your college connections, tutors and visiting staff, approach companies who may have sponsored college projects. Contact your peers and anyone else you know 'out there' in the industry who may be closer to the grapevine than you.
- Talk to people in industry – listen carefully and find out what they are requiring from employees.

- Offer to work for someone for free – for a few days or a week, for a few weeks or a month, to gain experience.
- Be prepared to do almost anything at first – to get your foot in the door – to have something to put on your CV.
- Don't be grand – many great careers start from humble beginnings.
- Be inventive, assess your skills and abilities and think where there may be someone who could use your talents.
- If you are going to work freelance or start your own business – get an accountant and talk to your bank manager.
- Get advice from the Crafts Council, Chartered Society of Designers or other appropriate professional bodies (see Useful addresses).

7 The future of art and design

The future of art and design looks healthy and exciting, and the boundaries of fine art are, as we have said earlier, continually breaking down in many instances and art is becoming the vehicle for our consciences, for our political ideas, and social comment. Often it is both the expression and the product of contemporary society. Similarly, design is expanding to embrace all areas of technology and contemporary life.

Design ideas are themselves perceived as marketable commercial products. They are used up and are superseded at an alarming rate. In contrast to this, we have the fringe movements (think of ecology and the green movement) that begin as reactionary and end up being part of mainstream thinking. Anti-fashion (punk) and the Indie music are two other examples.

The power of the media is made even more so since the global adoption of the Internet, bouncing ideas and information around the world. We are approaching the millennium and the world is changing ever more rapidly, jobs and employment patterns are changing also. In order to meet these challenges, education too must adapt and change, both to fulfil the desires of those in education and the needs of industry.

The revolutionary changes in communications mean that traditional work and education patterns are becoming impractical, outdated and unnecessary as the Internet means many people can work more from home and opens up opportunities for distance and home-based learning programmes.

Many educationalists are talking about large schools and colleges as dinosaurs, with ideas of 'a school on every corner' and having learning neighbourhoods. Other ideas are being discussed about lifelong learning, and taking the emphasis away from narrow specialisms (anti-specialisms) towards more diversity and more individualism. Economics and overcrowding in cities may mean a shift in focus from metropolitan life and even a blurring of definition between what we perceive as the country and the city.

It is interesting to speculate upon the future of art and design, but we can be certain of their integral places in future societies, and it may be up to you, the creative thinkers of the future to help shape the new millennium.

8 Useful addresses

Arts Councils

Arts Council of Great Britain, 14 Great Peter Street, London SW1P 3NQ; Tel: 0171 333 0100

Arts Council of Northern Ireland, 181 Stranmillis Road, Belfast BT9 5DU; Tel: 01232 381 591

Arts Council of Wales, Holst House, Museum Place, Cardiff CF1 3NX; Tel: 01222 394 711

Scottish Arts Council, 12 Manor Place, Edinburgh EH3 7DD; Tel: 0131 226 6051

Regional Arts Boards

Eastern Arts, Cherry Hinton Hall, Cherry Hinton Road, Cambridge CB1 4DW (Beds, Cambs, Essex, Herts, Lincs, Norfolk, Suffolk); Tel:01223 215 355

East Midlands Arts, Mountfields House, Forest Road, Loughbourgh, Leicester LE11 3HU (Northants, Derby, Leics, Notts); Tel: 01509 218 292

London Arts Board, Elme House, 133 Long Acre, London WC2E 9AF; Tel: 0171 240 1313

North West Art Board, 12 Harter Street, Manchester M16 6HY (Greater Manchester, Merseyside, Derbyshire, (high peak), Lancashire, Cheshire); Tel: 0161 228 3062

Northern Arts, 10 Osborne Terrace, Newcastle Upon Tyne NE2 1NZ (Tyne and Wear, Cleveland, Cumbria, Durham, Northumberland); Tel: 0191 281 6334

North Wales Arts, 10 Wellfield House, Bangor, Gwynedd LL57 1ER (Clwyd, Gwynedd, Montgomery district); Tel: 01248 353 248

South East Wales Arts Association, 9 Victoria Street, Cwmbran, Gwent NP4 3JP (Cardiff, Gwent, Mid-Glam, South Glam, Radnor, and Brecknock districts); Tel: 01633 875 075

South East Arts Board, 10 Mount Ephraim, Tunbridge Wells, Kent TN4 8AS (Kent, Surrey and Sussex); Tel: 01892 515 210

South West Arts, Bradninch Place, Gandy Street, Exeter, Devon EX4 2LS (Avon, Cornwall, Devon, Dorset except Bournemouth, Poole and Christchurch, Gloucestershire, Somerset); Tel: 01392 218 188

Southern Arts, 13 St Clement Street, Winchester SO23 9DQ (Berks, Bucks, Bournemouth, Poole and Christchurch, Isle of Wight, Hants, Oxon, W Sussex, Wilts); Tel: 01962 855 099

West Midland Arts, 82 Granville Street, Birmingham B1 2LH (Herefordshire, Worcestershire, West Midlands, Shropshire, Staffs, Warwicks); Tel: 0121 631 3121

Yorkshire and Humberside Arts, 21 Bond Street, Dewsbury, West Yorks WF13 1AX (Yorkshire, Humberside); Tel: 01924 455 555

Professional organizations, private colleges and other useful addresses

Acme Artists Housing Association Ltd, 44 Copperfield Row, London E3 4RR; Tel: 0181 981 6821

Advertising Association, Abford House, 15 Wilton Road, London SW1V 1NJ; Tel: 0171 828 2771

Arts Services Grants and Space, 6 & 8 Rosebery Avenue, London EC1R 4DT; Tel: 0171 278 5139

Art Workers Guild, 6 Queen Square, London WC1N 3AR; Tel: 0171 837 3474

Association of Artists and Designers in Wales, 54b Bute Street, Cardiff CF1 6AF; Tel: 01222 464 576

Association of British Picture Restorers, c/o Mrs Robinson, J H Cooke & Sons Ltd, Station Avenue, Richmond upon Thames, Surrey TW9 3QA; Tel: 0181 948 5644

Association of Exhibition Organisers, 26 Chapter Street, London SW1P 4ND; Tel: 0171 932 0252

Association of Illustrators, First Floor, 32–38 Saffron Hill, London EC1N 8FH; Tel: 0171 831 7377

BBC Corporate Recruitment Services, White City, Wood Lane, London W12 7TS; Tel: 0181 752 5252

Bristol Display Society, 70a Crayford High Street, Dartford, Kent DA1 4EF; Tel: 01322 550 544

Bristol Old Vic Theatre School, 1–2 Downside Road, Bristol BS8 2XF; Tel: 0117 987 7877

British Antique Dealers Association, 20 Rutland Gate, London SW7 1BD; Tel: 0171 589 4128

British Association of Art Therapists, 11a Richmond Road, Brighton, East Sussex BN2 3RL (an information folder costs £5; send sae for list)

British Council, 10 Spring Gardens, London SW1A 2BN; Tel: 0171 930 8466

British Film Institute, 21 Stephen Street, London W1P 2LN; Tel: 0171 255 1444

British Institute of Professional Photography, Fox Talbot House, Arnwell End, Ware, Herts SG12 5HN; Tel: 01920 464011

BTEC (Business and Technology Education Council), Central House, Upper Woburn Place, London WC1H OHH; Tel: 0171 413 8400

Byam Shaw School of Art, 2 Elthorne Road, London N19 4AG; Tel: 0181 281 4111

CAPITB Trust, 80 Richardshaw Lane, Pudsey, Leeds LS28 6BN; Tel: 0113 239 3355

Careers and Occupational Information Centre (COIC), Moorfoot, Sheffield S1 4PQ; Tel: 0114 259 4563

Careers Research and Advisory Centre (CRAC), Sheraton House, Castle Park, Cambridge CB3 OAX; Tel: 01233 460277

Central Services Unit for Careers and Appointments Services, Crawford House, Precinct Centre, Oxford Road, Manchester M13 9EP (for AGCAS careers literature and vacancy information for graduates); Tel: 0161 237 5409

Chartered Society of Designers, 32 – 38 Saffron Hill, London ECI 8FH; Tel: 0171 831 9777

Christie's, 63 Old Brompton Road, London SW7 3JS; Tel: 0171 581 3933

City and Guilds of London Institute, 1 Giltspur Street, London EC1A 9DD; Tel: 0171 294 2468

Communication, Advertising and Marketing Education Foundation, Abford House, 15 Wilton Road, London SW1V INJ; Tel: 0171 828 7506

Computer Arts Society, PO Box 1454, Station Road, Swindon SN1 1TG; Tel: 01793 480269

Council for British Archaeology, Bowes Morrell House, 111 Walmgate, York YO1 2UA; Tel: 01904 671417

Crafts Council, 44a Pentonville Road, London N1 9HF; Tel: 0171 278 7700

Design Council, 1 Oxenden Street, London SW1 1Y; Tel: 0171 208 2121

Design Council (Scotland), Ca d'Oro Building, 45 Gordon Street, Glasgow G1 3LZ

Design Council (Wales), QED Centre, Main Avenue, Treforest Estate, Treforest, Pontypridd CF37 5TR

Designers and Art Directors Annual, 9 Graphite Square, Vauxhall Walk, London SE11 5EE; Tel: 0171 582 6487

Graphic, Paper and Media Union, 9 Newburgh Street, London W1V 1LH; Tel: 0171 587 1315 (enquiries)

Independent Television Commission (ITC), 33 Foley Street, London W1P 7LB; Tel: 0171 255 3000

Independant Schools Joint Coucil, Grovenor Gardens House, Grovenor Gardens, London SW1 1PS; Tel: 0171 630 0144

Institute of Medical Illustrators, c/o Angus Robertson, Medical and Dental Illustration Unit, Leeds Dental Institute, Clarendon Way, Leeds LS2 9LU; Tel: 0113 233 6258

Institute of Packaging, Sysonby Lodge, Nottingham Road, Melton Mowbray, Leics LE13 ONU; Tel: 01664 500055

Institute of Practitioners in Advertising, 44 Belgrave Square, London SW1X 8QS; Tel: 0171 235 7020

Institute of Scientific and Technical Communicators, Kings Court, 2 – 16 Goodge Street, London W1P 1FF; Tel: 0171 436 4425

London Enterprise Agency, (Design Enterprise Programme), 4 Snow Hill, London EC1A 2BS; Tel: 0171 236 3000

Museums Association, 42 Clerkenwell Close, London EC1R 0PA; Tel: 0171 608 2933

National Artists' Association, Interchange Studios, Dalby Street, London NW5 3NQ; Tel: 0171 426 0911

National Association of Decorative and Fine Arts Societies, 8a Lower Grosvenor Place, London SW1W 0EN; Tel: 0171 233 5433

National Council for Vocational Qualifications, 222 Euston Road, London NW1 2BZ; Tel: 0171 387 9898

National Society for Education in Art and Design, The Gatehouse, Corsham Court, Corsham SN13 0BZ; Tel: 01249 14825

The Prince's Trust, 6 Gilpin Road, London E5 (outreach office) or, 227a City Road, London EC1 (London Division volunteers); Tel: 0800 842 842 (enquiries)

Riverside Studios, Crisp Road, London W6 9RL; Tel: 0181 741 2251

Royal College of Art, Kensington Gore, London SW7 2EU; Tel: 0171 584 5020

Rural Development Commission, 141 Castle Street, Salisbury, Wiltshire; Tel: 01722 336 255

SCOTVEC (Scottish Vocational Education Council), Hanover House, 24 Douglas Street, Glasgow G2 7NQ; Tel: 0141 248 7900

The Shelton Trust, (Community Arts), The Old Tin School, Collihurst Road, Manchester M10 7RQ

Society of Designer Craftsmen, 24 Rivington Street, London EC2A 3DU; Tel: 0171 739 3663

Society of Scottish Artists, 69 Promenade, Portobello, Edinburgh EH15 2DX; Tel: 0131 669 0637

Society of Typographic Designers, 21-27 Seagrave Road, London SW6 1RP; Tel: 0171 381 4258

Sotherby's Works of Art Course, 30 Oxford Street, London W1R 1RE; Tel: 0171 323 5775

Student Loans Company

Textile Conservation Centre Ltd, Hampton Court Place, East Molesey, Surrey KT8 9AU; Tel: 0181 977 4943

Textile Institute, 10 Blackfriars Street, Manchester M3 5DR; Tel: 0161 834 8457

United Kingdom Institute for the Conservation and Restoration of Historic and Artistic Works, 6 Whitehorse Mews, Westminster Bridge Road, London SE1 7QD; Tel: 0171 620 3771

Clearing houses for courses

Clearing House for Postgraduate Courses in Art and Design, Penn House, 9 Broad Street, Hereford HR4 9EP; Tel: 01432 266 653

Graduate Teacher Training Registry, Fulton House, Jessop Avenue, Cheltenham, Gloucestershire GL50 3SH; Tel: 01242 225 868

TEACH (Teacher Education Admissions Clearing House), PO Box 165, Holyrood Road, Edinburgh EH8 8AT; Tel: 0131 558 6170

UCAS, Fulton House, Jessop Avenue, Cheltenham, Gloucestershire GL50 3SH; Application enquiries Tel: 01242 227 788; Website http: www.ucas.ac.uk

9 Further reading

The addresses of organizations and publishers are listed below.

Course directories

Careers Research and Advisory Centre, *Degree Course Guide: Art and Design*. Lists courses in art and design and the history of craft and art. Updated annually.

Design Council, *Design Courses*. Starting point for those considering the study of a craft discipline. Describes courses from preparatory to postgraduate level, including teacher education. Updated annually.

Education and Training for Film and Television

Scottish Universities' Entrance Guide, Scottish Universities' Council on Entrance,

Stallard, M *The Art and Design Directory*, AVEC Designs. Gives details of first degree, HND and DipHE courses in art, design and communications. Updated annually.

UCAS, *UCAS Handbook*. Updated annually.

Newpoint Publishing Ltd. *Which Degree?*

Grants

Grant booklets are available from your local education authority and from:

Department for Education and Employment, Honeypot Lane, Canons Park, Stanmore, Middlesex HA7 1AZ

Scottish Education Department, Awards Branch, Gyleview House, 3 Redheughs Rigg, South Gyle, Edinburgh EH12 9HH

Department of Education for Northern Ireland, Rathgael House, Balloo Road, Bangor BT19 2PR

Useful publications

AGCAS Careers Booklets. *Fine Art, Fashion and Textile Design, Two and Three-dimensional Design.*

Art World Directory, and Art Review – for gallery addresses.

Association of Illustrators, *Survive.*

A & C Black, *Writers' and Artists' Yearbook,* directory of newspapers, magazines, articles on finding an agency, copyright, self - marketing, updated annually.

British Association of Art Therapies Ltd, leaflets on art therapy.

British Qualifications (1995) Kogan Page, London.

Careers Occupational Information Centre (1993) *Working in Art and Design.*

Chapman, N (1997) *Careers in Fashion*, Kogan Page, London.

Charlton, T (1985) *Guide to Courses and Careers in Art, Craft and Design*, National Society for Education in Art and Design.

Department for Education and Employment, *Guide to Grants: Postgraduate Awards*, Postgraduate Awards Division, HFE3, Honeypot Lane, Stanmore, Middx HA7 1AZ.

Student Grants and Loans. Free booklet from Department for Education and Employment.

Crafts Council, *Running a Workshop* basic business for craftspeople.

Crocker, M *Guide to First Degree and Postgraduate Courses in Fashion and Textile Design*, available from Department of Fashion and Textiles, University of Central England, in Birmingham, Corporation Street, Birmingham B4 7DX.

Crowe, J and Stokes, J (1998) *Art, Design and Crafts: A Manual*

for Business Success, Hodder and Stoughton, London.
Golzen, G (1997) *Working for Yourself*, Kogan Page, London.
Goslett, D (1983) *The Professional Practice of Design*, Batsford, London.
London Art and Artists Guide, galleries and sources of information.
Museums and Arts Galleries in Great Britain, a directory published by The Museums Association, gives a comprehensive guide to the collections and the museums and galleries where they are housed.
Museums Association, *Careers in Museums*, available on request.
Reed Information Services, *The Creative Handbook* – a directory of design consultancies, illustrators, advertising agencies, etc. updated annually.
Reed Information Services, *Museums and Galleries in GB.*
Reed Information Services, *Willings Press Guide,* lists newspapers and periodicals.
Richardson, J (1998) *Careers in Theatre*, Kogan Page, London.
Selby, M (1997) *Careers in Television and Radio*, Kogan Page, London.
The Textile Institute, various publications and course lists.
United Kingdom Institute for the Conservation and Restoration of Historic and Artistic Works, *Careers in Conservation and Restoration.*

Journals and periodicals

Regular reading of the periodicals relevant to your interest is essential for keeping in touch with new developments, events, exhibitions, jobs and companies or consultancies or design groups you might want to work for.

The national press, such as *The Times, The Guardian* (creative and media appointments), *Daily Telegraph, Daily Mail*, the *Sunday Times, Observer, Sunday Telegraph*, the *Independent*, also advertise jobs in art and design, as do local newspapers from time to time. But you may find that some of the specialist journals are the best and sometimes the only places in which to start your search for a job or to build your list of potential employers.

Key: W = weekly M = monthly Q = quarterly
A selection of those particularly useful to artists and designers is given below. Items marked ⋆ are obtainable from newsagents.

Artist's Newsletter (M) job ads, bursaries, competitions, grants, news, reviews: for visual artists. AN Publications, PO Box 23, Sunderland SR1 1BR.

Association of Illustrators Newsletter (M).

Campaign⋆ (W) advertising, graphic design and other posts in design consultancies, publishing, arts, media, and marketing

City Limits⋆(W) community arts, arts, mainly London.

Crafts (bi-M) the magazine for the artist and craftsperson; some vacancies, bursaries, workshop space. Available from the Crafts Council.

Current Vacancies (M) posts generally open to graduates from university careers in all disciplines – some in the arts services Central Services Unit, Crawford House, Precinct Centre, Oxford Road, Manchester M13 9EP.

D Magazine (3 times a year), Gillard, Welch Ltd, Chester Court, High Street, Knowle, Solihull B99 0LL.

Design Week (W) design appointments, St Giles House, 50 Poland Street, London W1V 4AX.

Drapers Record ⋆ 'DR' (W) fashion and textile design, manufacture, retail/wholesale trade.

Fashion Weekly ⋆ (W) fashion design and production posts.

Illustrators (Q) Magazine of the Association of Illustrators.

Knitting International ⋆ (M) Knitwear design – some appointments in design and production.

Museum Bulletin (M) all posts in national and provincial museums and art galleries. Journal of the Museums Association includes keepers, designers, conservators.

The Stage and Television Today ⋆ (W) posts in theatre.

Time Out ⋆ (W) arts, community projects, media – mostly Greater London.

The Times Educational Supplement ⋆ (W) teaching posts in schools, colleges, higher education, remedial and art therapy.

The Times Higher Education Supplement ⋆ (W).

Index

HAVERING COLLEGE OF F & H E
19997